THE COLLECTED
PHILOSOPHICAL PAPERS OF
G. E. M. ANSCOMBE

III   Ethics, Religion and Politics

THE COLLECTED
PHILOSOPHICAL PAPERS OF
G. E. M. ANSCOMBE

VOLUME THREE

Ethics, Religion and Politics

University of Minnesota Press · Minneapolis

Published by the University of Minnesota Press,
2037 University Avenue Southeast, Minneapolis MN 55414
Printed in Great Britain

Library of Congress Cataloging in Publication Data

Anscombe, G. E. M. (Gertrude Elizabeth Margaret)
  Ethics, religion, and politics.

  (The collected philosophical papers of
G. E. M. Anscombe; v. 3)
  Includes index.
  Contents: The two kinds of error in action –
On promising and its justice, and whether it needs
be respected in foro interno – On brute facts –
[etc.]
  1. Ethics – Addresses, essays, lectures.
2. Religion – Philosophy – Addresses, essays,
lectures   3. Political science – Addresses,
essays, lectures.   I. Title.   II. Series: Anscombe,
G. E. M. (Gertrude Elizabeth Margaret). Essays; v. 3.
B1618.A571   1981, vol. 3 [BJ1012] 192s [170] 81-4315
ISBN 0-8166-1082-7   AACR2
ISBN 0-8166-1083-5 (pbk.)

The University of Minnesota
is an equal-opportunity
educator and employer.

Contents

Introduction

Some of the papers in this volume – numbers 1–4, 7, 10, 13 and 14 – were written for the general public, for ordinary philosophical meetings or for philosophical journals. Others – numbers 5, 6, 9, 11, 12 – were composed to express an explicitly Catholic view; indeed they were mostly written for meetings of Catholics or were addressed to a Catholic readership. This accounts for a difference of assumptions. For, addressing Catholics or writing expressly as a Catholic, I would assume a certain background of common belief and faith, and might or might not discuss these in their problematic aspects. There is one paper, number 8, which straddles the two classifications. It is the part which I wrote of a pamphlet called "The Justice of the Present War Examined", the second part of which was written by my friend Norman Daniel. We were both undergraduates at Oxford at the time and we gave our pamphlet an extra description as expressing a 'Catholic view'; we got it on sale in Oxford bookshops and, I think, in one or two London ones. Soon the University Chaplain sent for Norman Daniel and told him the Archbishop of Birmingham wanted us to withdraw it: we had no right to call it 'Catholic' without getting an *imprimatur*. (Bishops *seemed* to have much more authority in those days.) We obeyed: we thought the demand wrong and unreasonable, but the authority of one's ordinary involved the right to exercise such control. Some notice of the pamphlet had got into the press, and it seems this had alarmed the Archbishop.

I include my share of this pamphlet in this collection because it has a certain historical interest: it shows some truths which it was possible to judge about the war already in the autumn of 1939. When in 1956 I opposed the conferment of an honorary degree by Oxford University on Mr Truman, Mr Goodhart, then Master of University College, sneered at my 'hindsight' about the conduct of the war by the massacre of civilian populations: the pamphlet shows that this was already seen by us as what was going to happen, and as lying in the intentions of our rulers, in 1939. – My remarks about the 'injustice' of the Treaty of Versailles were, I fear, a mere repetition of the common propaganda of the day. I hadn't read the treaty and had no right to echo that widely purveyed opinion.

"War and Murder", number 6, was written for a collection of Catholic essays and, while expressing the same general moral opinions as the other two pieces (numbers 7 and 8) is written in a tone of righteous fury about what passed for thinking about the destruction of civilian populations. I don't much like it, not because I disagree with its sentiments but because, if I was torn by a *saeva indignatio*, I wish I had had the talent of Swift in expressing it.

I would have said I got interested in political philosophy in the 1970s, simply out of an interest in the concept of murder. 'Murder' is a moral action concept of great complexity, and one cannot give an account of it without discussing both whether its definition *includes* its wrongfulness, and *also* whether and why capital punishment and some other deliberate killings under the authority of the state do not fall under the concept 'murder'. But I see the seeds of my interest in political theory were there in the writings about war, though I did not then refer to civil authority in a questioning or even enquiring spirit.

In general, my interest in moral philosophy has been more in particular moral questions than in what is now called 'meta-ethics'. (The analogous thing is unrestrictedly true about philosophy of religion, as may be seen from papers 11 and 12 in this collection.) So far as general questions of moral theory have interested me, I have thought them closely tied up with problems of action-description and unsettlable without help from philosophy of mind. Some of these papers represent a struggle to treat all deliberate action as a matter of acting on a calculation how to obtain one's ends. I have now become rather doubtful about this. Of course, it is always possible to force practical reasons into this mould, constructing descriptions of ends like "not infringing the regulations about traffic lights", "observing the moral law", "being polite", "playing a game according to its rules", and so on. But it now seems to me that there is a contrast between such constructed descriptions of ends, and the means–ends calculations which really do – at least implicitly – take their starting point from some objective which one has. Certain considerations put before me by my friend Georg Henrik von Wright have led me to think this; but I have no full-fledged thoughts on the subject, and what I publish is, I think, all written under the older conception.

The paper on contraception is a first version of a paper which I published in a rather more developed form in *The Human World*: here it excited attack from my colleagues Bernard Williams and Michael Tanner, as well as some friendlier criticism from Peter Winch. It was eventually published with some small revisions by the Catholic Truth Society as a pamphlet under the title "Contraception and Chastity". That final form is not much different in substance from the original paper delivered at the Conference of Theological Renewal, which met in Toronto in 1966 to celebrate the bicentenary of Canada. I wouldn't think the difference of sufficient interest to publish both texts here. The first version, which I do publish here, is perhaps argued more delicately and problematically. It also has the historical interest of being delivered before *Human Vitae* came out. In it I wished my audience to draw for itself what seemed to me the obvious conclusion: namely that you might as well accept any sexual goings-on, if you accepted contraceptive intercourse. At that time this was denied by the 'Catholic' defenders of contraception, though it has since been cheerfully embraced. I also thought then that the promotion of contraception by having public clinics might prevent the far worse business of widespread abortion. This used to be argued; but I very soon came to think it an illusion. Only in countries where abortion was already much practised, and contraceptives not easy to get, did a new availability of contraceptives reduce abortion; and the reduction was only temporary. Abortion has indeed now come to be regarded as a long-stop for unwanted conceptions and a desirable means of population control. One could say: if you want to promote abortion, promote contraception. We now live in a kind of madness on these themes, in which vocal people at large are completely thoughtless about the awful consequences of *far less than reproducing* the parental generation, where it has itself been a large one. Our schools are already suffering, as professional teachers know, and what they can offer in the way of specialist teaching, such as the teaching of music, for example, is being cut down. Nor is it difficult to smell prospective murder in the air: so far, we have the murder of defective infants, but among young doctors we hear mutterings about the senile occupancy of valuable beds. These are likely to be echoes of what is said among the older members of the profession.

Part One

Ethics

1   The Two Kinds of Error in Action

The jurisprudent Glanville Williams derides the maxim "Fraud vitiates consent".

> Consent [he says] is a psychological fact. It is not a mere legal concept, like a right; it is a fact, though a fact having legal consequences. This being so, it is impossible for fraud to vitiate (in the sense of 'destroy') consent. If consent once exists, fraud cannot destroy it . . . any more than it can take the roof off a house. Fraud can destroy rights, for they are merely things of the imagination, and we can imagine them as destroyed whenever we like; but it cannot destroy facts . . . Regarded as a proposition of fact, therefore, the maxim that fraud vitiates consent is untrue, and not all the authority of the highest court in England can make it true. What the judges have the power to say is only that fraud shall vitiate consent *as a matter of law*, or, expressing the proposition more clearly, that fraud shall destroy (not consent but) the legal effects that would otherwise follow from consent.[1]

This author regards the statement that fraud vitiates consent as it would be correct to regard a statement that fraud (in eliciting it) vitiates a blush.

His mistake is obvious. Consent is consent to something. Thus there may be consent to one thing that one has done, such as putting one's signature on a piece of paper that is proffered to one, and yet not to another thing that one has done, such as putting one's signature to a property transfer. The document proffered to the signatory, we will suppose, actually is a property transfer; but he has it read to him (as he thinks) because his sight is impaired. What *is* read out to him is only a petition for someone's reprieve, and that is what he thinks he is signing.

Thus "fraud vitiates consent" is a maxim that has application only where there *is* consent to *something*; but if we hear of "consent to what occurred", then we ought to ask: How do you mean, *to what occurred?* i.e. "consent to what occurred *under what description?*" Under the description "signing the document presented by so-and-so" there was consent to what took place; under the description "signing a transfer of property" there was not. Naturally the case in which Glanville Williams ran foul of the maxim was far more disputable than this; otherwise he could hardly have made that mistake. (It was a case of handing over a parcel to an impostor.)

To be sure, fraud cannot nullify any actual psychological fact of consent. But, because consent is consent to something and you may consent to something under one description and not under another, the fact of fraud may be a proof that a *certain* consent has not taken place at all. That is the ground of the legal maxim. Constraint, or not having had anything to do

[1] *Canadian Bar Review*, 23, pp. 281 ff.

From *Journal of Philosophy*, 60 (1963).

with the matter, are thus not the only possible grounds for denying that one consented to something.

We could enlarge the maxim, in moral philosophy, to "Error destroys action". The distinction between raising one's hand and signifying that one wants to speak, when one signifies that one wants to speak by raising one's hand, is parallel to the distinction in the signing case between signing one's name on the proffered document and transferring one's property.

What bearing can what the agent thinks have on the true description of what he does? Someone may want to say: if what he does is a happening, a physical event, something 'in the external world', then that happening must be something that takes place, whatever the agent thinks. If you give a description of it, for the truth of which it matters what the agent thinks, such as "He got married", "He swore on oath", "He murdered his father", then your description ought to be broken down into descriptions of thoughts and of purely physical happenings.

If we ask: Why? the answer is: because what an agent thinks simply cannot make any difference to the truth of a description of a physical fact or event.

But, if you say this, it only shows what you mean by "a physical fact or event". A physical transaction is being taken to be one for which this holds: what a party to it thinks is indifferent. But then so far nothing substantial has been said by saying that a murder or a wedding that has taken place is not a physical fact or that "a murder" or "a wedding" is not a physical description; for "physical" has been *defined* in terms of the irrelevance of thought.

In some contexts it would sound absurd to deny that a murder or wedding which took place was a physical fact.

It is characteristic of these and many other descriptions 'X' of human actions that one can ask: "In doing what was he X-ing?" For example, by pronouncing such-and-such words in such-and-such circumstances one gets married. That is why it is possible for ignorance or lack of intent to vitiate consent or nullify an action of a certain description. For example, one thought one was rehearsing a wedding ceremony. In that case the lack of intent means that one has not got married at all, just as in the fraud case it meant that one had not transferred one's property.

There are some descriptions 'X' of things done that cannot hold unless the subject knows he is doing X; for example, making a contract. There are some that can hold though the subject does not know he is doing X; for example, signing a transfer. But there are, further, some interesting intermediate cases.

Examples of what I have in mind would be adultery, murder, bigamy. Suppose a man lives with a woman whom he has every reason to believe he has married, but in fact she was married to someone else and so, by the institutions in which he lives, not to him. Has he committed adultery? If so, certainly he has done so unwittingly and unintentionally. Now, some might be inclined to say: he committed adultery without knowing it, and some: he did not really commit adultery. The latter are using "adultery" as everyone uses "stealing": that, we say, was not stealing; the man reasonably thought the property his own.

Here it is helpful to introduce the old distinction between the formal and the material as in "formal and material object" of, say, shooting. You shoot, as you think, at a stag; what you thought was a stag turns out to be a man. In one sense – the formal – your object was a stag; in the other – the material – it was a man. Returning to our putatively married man, there is no dispute about one level of description. The facts and the relevant actions, under one description, are quite clear. Dispute whether to speak of involuntary, and so innocent, adultery or to say that it wasn't adultery at all should be settled by the formula: materially, but not formally, he committed adultery.

Now we may notice that the terms "murder" and "theft" are so used that formality is essential to them; it is built into their meaning – unless, possibly, in face of a special question we shall be coming to later. If a man genuinely and reasonably, but wrongly, thought that this was property he had a right to take away, then we say "That was not stealing at all".

Nevertheless there is a contrast between actions of the type of making contracts and such actions as murder. You have to think you are making a contract in order to be doing so, whereas you do not have to think that what you do is murder in order for it to be murder. What is necessary for your action to be murder is that you deliberately do such-and-such; this entails that you know you are doing such-and-such. Murder, however, is a very special concept, as is seen from the distinction between it and other forms of culpable homicide.

There is thus a further contrast between such an act as murder and actions performable without knowing that you are doing that to do which *is* to do them. Indeed very many offences fall in this class. I will take bigamy as an example. "I acted in good faith in marrying Jane, for I did not know that my first wife, Mary, was still alive" could hardly be a successful plea if the speaker had no strong grounds for supposing his wife dead, but had acted on the assumption that his first marriage would never come to light. In particular, if he made no inquiry and especially if a simple inquiry would have revealed that his wife was alive, the plea of good faith would be positively refuted. Thus he went through a marriage ceremony in circumstances such that he materially committed bigamy. He did not know those circumstances; nevertheless it was both possible and necessary for him to ascertain them, and hence his lack of knowledge and of positive intent do not exonerate him. So bigamy can be formally imputed to him.

This situation is likely to be particularly provided for in a society with an advanced legal system. I refer to such provisions as that a man must seek leave to presume death. What I have said thus relates to the situation existing before such provisions and for the sake of which such provisions exist.

For other misdeeds, such as adultery and theft, there are hardly any such provisions, either because the positive law is not interested or because the matter of the offence is not so sweepingly tractable. (One doesn't marry very often and it is a very definite action, but dealing with people's property is much more various and frequent.) But it is possible to be *guilty* of adultery without knowing that one is doing what, materially speaking, is adultery if, say, one does not bother to find out whether one's partner is married. This might be one of Aristotle's cases of ἀκρασία: we suppose an unmarried man who strongly disapproves of adultery, but is so vehemently tempted that, without consideration, he commits adultery with someone he has recently met at a party.

We have noticed that you don't have to think of your action as a murder for it to be a murder. You do have to think (rightly) that you are doing such-and-such – say, putting deadly poison in your husband's soup; then when he dies of it you have committed murder. This is the doctrine of the *mens rea*, which has misled some: for they think that "a guilty mind" must mean "a mind conscious of evil-doing", so that someone who thought himself justified would not have a guilty mind (see a footnote in H. L. A. Hart's Presidential Address to the Aristotelian Society). This, however, is a mis-understanding no doubt deriving from the widepsread modern moral doctrine that a man who acts according to his conscience cannot be guilty of wrong-doing. The older doctrine, however, both in law and in morals, was that, however proper a man thought it to-kill-this-person-in-these-circumstances, if the law (presumed to be a just one) does not permit him to kill that man or to kill anyone in such circumstances, then he is proved to have a guilty intent once it is shown that what he intended was: to kill-this-person-in-these-circumstances. Whereas a mistake, such that if things were as he thought the law would permit the killing, proves that the requisite *mens rea* was not present. For example, to take a plain-sailing example, if he were a public executioner, and, without his connivance, the wrong man got presented to him to execute.

Now I said: if a man genuinely and reasonably (but wrongly) thought he had a right to take possession of certain property, that would not be stealing. But the condition is ambiguous. It might mean: "If a man wrongly, but genuinely and reasonably, thought that the circumstances were cir-cumstances *XYZ* and if in circumstances *XYZ* he would have the right to take possession, then this would not be stealing"; or it might mean: "If a man were right enough as to the circumstances but erroneously, though genuinely and reasonably, thought that *in those circumstances* he had the right . . .". The one case is that of ignorance of fact, the other ignorance of law.

It seems that positive coded law can't take account of ignorance of law, except by providing for conditions of special promulgation to certain classes of people, without which they are not to be liable to penalty. Legal and juridical practice can and does – by abstention from prosecutions, by letting off with a warning, by light sentences. When we turn from law to morality, it looks as if we need a theory of the matter. For it would seem absurd to maintain that *only* error as to facts could exonerate, error as to right and wrong never, and yet equally absurd to maintain that the latter sort of error always exonerated. The doctrines that you can't help what you think and that thoughts that such-and-such is right or wrong aren't characterizable as truth or error have conspired to prevent this question from being much considered. I don't hold either doctrine, and so the question strikes me as interesting and important.

Exoneration means that the action of, say, theft is not imputed to the subject. Good faith (which I take it is more than really thinking such-and-such, more than just not having your tongue in your cheek) does exonerate. This means that it is easy to see how mistakes on matters of fact may prevent an action from being of such-and-such a character. If something, call it S, has to be voluntarily done-in-circumstances-C in order to be a certain action A, then blameless ignorance of C proves that the agent did not do A. But when we consider error about whether doing S in circumstances C *is* doing A, it is very difficult to show the rationale of A's not being imputable to the agent. For he did voluntarily, even intentionally,[2] do S in circumstances C.

A famous example is that of the public executioner who has private knowledge of a condemned man's innocence. In some way he knows he cannot make use of it to get the man off; and he is to execute him. The man had a fair trial. The question is whether it is, morally speaking, an act of murder for the executioner, at the command of his superiors, to perform his office in these circumstances. Doctors have disagreed about this. It is clearly a very difficult question. It seems unavoidable to say that, if the executioner is concerned with the question as one of conscience, forms a *bona fide* judgement that he can or should execute the man, and acts accordingly, then murder cannot be imputed to him. Suppose there is a right decision, and suppose – for the sake of the argument merely – his is wrong. Then won't the formal-material distinction come into play even in the case of murder? For the question the executioner is asking is not one that he can answer on the grounds that he is considering the question conscientiously!

Once more, what is the rationale of the possibility that ignorance of law, as opposed to fact, should exonerate? From Aristotle (*Nicomachean Ethics*, 1113b33–1114a1) on, the best writers have held that, where it was easy to know the law, then there is no possibility of exoneration: good faith in ignorance is here excluded. The rationale, then, directly concerns the difficulty of the question. But it will take some further analysis to lay it bare.

It will aid this analysis to remember an amusing passage from Hume's *Treatise* about accusing trees of parricide: "'Tis not sufficient to reply that choice or will is wanting. For in the case of parricide a will does not give rise to any different relations but is only the cause from which the action was derived."

What a rule forbids is often *the doing of such-and-such*. When, however, you

---

[2] The difference between voluntariness and intentionalness that I here refer to is this: one cannot intentionally, but can voluntarily, do something without knowing one is doing it; e.g. some voluntary cases are like those of bigamy and adultery when the agent made no inquiry.

have done such-and-such, the question whether you are *guilty* of doing such-and-such is not simply a question about what exteriorly happened, but about your will. Naturally, a rule as you consider it in deciding to obey or disobey it does not run: do not *voluntarily* do such-and-such, for you cannot consider whether to do such-and-such voluntarily or not. So even when the notion of *a guilty performance*, *if any*, is built into the description of the forbidden thing (as with stealing or murder, though not with adultery), what a man considers is whether to take this horse or this money or whether to kill this other man, not whether to do so voluntarily. The voluntariness is presupposed in his *considering whether* to do so. Thus it does not come into his considerations of what to do, but it does come into a later judgement – his own or another's – of what was done.

Now voluntariness is relative to description of action. And just as the maxim "fraud vitiates consent" has application only where there is consent to something, so my maxim "error destroys action" has application only where there is *some* voluntary action. You do such-and-such, but your ignorance of circumstances C prevents your doing such-and-such from being a case of doing A, or of voluntarily doing A – which we say will depend on whether guiltiness is built into the description A or not. It is simplest to suppose a case in which it is not. Now I got into a difficulty through wrongly making the following inference: if doing A just is doing S in circumstances C, then voluntarily doing S in circumstances C is voluntarily doing A. That this doesn't *have* to follow is clear from the parallel: from "doing A just is doing S in circumstances C" it doesn't follow that knowing you are doing S in circumstances C is knowing you are doing A.

I was thrown off the scent, being confused by the fact that *knowledge* is not necessary for voluntariness; where ignorance is due to carelessness, the man did A voluntarily though he didn't know he was doing A. That is true enough, but does not show that one can always infer from "voluntarily did S in circumstances C" to "voluntarily did A". Now we have to ask: "What is the rationale of *ever* holding a man guilty when he is ignorant?" The answer must be: the ignorance is sometimes voluntary.

Let us compare the will as agent to the pilot of a ship. The loss of the ship is ascribed to the pilot not merely if he does certain things but also if he doesn't do certain things – as the spoiling of potatoes is ascribed to the cook's *failure* to put salt in them. So, sometimes, because of what a man's will *doesn't* do, he acts in ignorance, and the resultant happening-with-him-as-subject is imputable to him. For example, say, he simply fails to consider the iniquity of a law deeming that Jews or unborn babies are not human, and he co-operates in their killing. Thus, as a means to an end or as an end in itself, he joined in the killing of the innocent. But that would be a good explanation of the *central* idea of murder, unjust killing of humans.

Now when the happening-with-A-as-subject is described by the explanation of an offence X – say murder – then X will be imputable to A when he is ignorant that doing the thing in question is *X*, only if his ignorance is voluntary.

When will this be so? The answer is to be seen from the cases of the pilot and the cook: when it was necessary and possible for him to know, then the ignorance is voluntary, just as when it was necessary and possible for the pilot to navigate and for the cook to put salt in the potatoes, the loss of the ship and the spoiling of the potatoes are ascribed to the pilot and cook as causes. (Various senses of "possible" and of "ascribed . . . as causes" are possible here.) So when it was necessary and possible for *A* to know, the ignorance is ascribed to *A*'s will as cause.

"Necessity" here has a sense little examined by philosophers, but given by Aristotle in his dictionary *Metaphysics Δ*. Things are in this sense necessary when without them some good can't be got or some evil avoided. This necessity is present anyway in all these cases. The pilot must navigate to preserve the ship; the cook must put salt in the potatoes to cook them well; *A* very likely must know what is just and unjust for him to do if he is to avoid acting unjustly. (To simplify the case, we will suppose there is an offence against justice on *A*'s part in disobeying his orders, *if* it is not positively unjust to obey them.)

But the possibility of knowledge may be lacking, because of the difficulty of the question. Thus the rationale of being exonerated by ignorance of principle is itself the same as that of being exonerated by ignorance of fact. But the topic is more difficult because of the Hume point about parricide: *what* one describes the action as, when considering what is, e.g., forbidden does not bring in the conditions of imputability. The context requires that what one is saying is good or bad to do be voluntary actions – and anything that proves that *under such and such a description* what took place was not the subject's voluntary action will affect what can be *imputed* to him. The topic is further complicated by the fact that imputability of some actions, like murder, is built into the meanings of their names.

When I discussed these matters at the APA meeting in Columbus, Ohio, Professor Joel Feinberg objected that "murder" was a legal concept, so that he did not know what I was at. I replied that this is often said, but only because it is said, and the best thing to do about it is to stop saying it. No one, for example, concerns himself with questions of legality before calling "murder" the killings of so many people by the Hitler regime. To say that what is and what is not unjust killing of men is purely a matter of what the law allows and forbids is the positivism of Thrasymachus,[3] which has not the right to behave as if it were the merest common sense, difficult to reject.

---

[3] See G. Hourani, "Thrasymachus' Definition of Justice in Plato's *Republic*", *Phronesis*, 7, 2 (1962), pp. 110–12. Hourani argues very convincingly that a definition of justice as obeying the laws is assumed by Thrasymachus.

2 On Promising and its Justice, and Whether it Need be Respected *in Foro Interno*

Whether or not there are any human actions which take place purely within the soul – and whatever it may mean to say or deny that there are – there are at any rate many, many actions which are exterior happenings. If one human beats or kisses another, if he makes a box or walks or turns a crank or . . . or . . . – there is no need to continue the list which could be indefinitely extended – these would be unhesitatingly called actions, at least in normal contexts; and also they are happenings, physical events. A question which is all-important for our investigation is this: what bearing can what the agent thinks have on the description of the action? If the action is a physical happening, someone may want to say that a physical happening is what takes place, whatever the agent thinks.

Such things as marrying, making a gift, swearing an oath seem to be counter-examples. It is essential to getting married, as it is to the other things, that someone who is doing it should think he is doing it.

Two questions arise about this type of case. First, how is it possible? And second, does it provide genuine counter-examples?

For, first, there seems to be a logical difficulty. If thinking you are getting married is essential to getting married, then mention of thinking you are getting married belongs in an explanation of what getting married is; but then won't an explanation of what getting married is be required if we are to give the content of thought that one is getting married? Hence it will be impossible to explain what getting married is and impossible to say what is the thought of the man who thinks he is getting married; and so generally for all cases of this type.

It might seem that where "p" is a statement such as "A is getting married", "A is making a contract", etc., then we are wrongly inclined to say that the truth of "A thinks that p" is an essential component of the truth of "p" in any paradoxical sense; the true explanation of "p" must be "q" and "A thinks that q", where "q" states the other conditions for the truth of "p", which can hold whether or no A thinks they hold. That is, in all these actions there is the physical happening and the mental component. We might then get rid of the paradox, thus: suppose it is granted that if a man thinks something he also thinks (i.e. believes) that he thinks it. Then if q and A thinks that q, he also thinks that q and that he thinks that q, i.e. he thinks that

p. This would explain why it can be the case that p only if A thinks that p, without paradox.

This explanation, however, will not do. Firstly, even if p.q=r, "A thinks that p and thinks that q" does not necessarily imply "A thinks that r". Secondly, a set of circumstances may hold, adequate for it to be true that a marriage is taking place, apart from this one point – that one of the parties does not think that what they are doing is getting married – and both parties may know that set of circumstances, which would otherwise be adequate. To give an example, we might suppose that one of the parties has mis-understood someone's remark "This is only a rehearsal" as referring to the imminent procedure. Thus the thought that q cannot take the place of the thought that p, and we are left with the fact that for such interpretations of "p" "A thinks that p" is an indispensable verifier of "p", a precondition, not a mere consequence of "p". The difficulty about it must then be illusory, and an opinion about the relations between thought and what happens, from which it follows that this situation is impossible, must be false. To be sure, to say this is not to dispel the difficulty. But I will return to that later.

My second question was: does this type of case provide genuine counter-examples to the thesis that, if an action that takes place is a physical happen-ing, that physical happening is what takes place, whatever the agent thinks?

Someone may want to say: "these are not genuine counter-examples, because, e.g., the making of a contract is not a physical fact but, say, a legal fact. And it is only for a physical fact that it holds that if it comes about, it comes about whatever the agent thinks." He might add that it will no doubt turn out to be some peculiarity of such things as legal facts that accounts for the difficulty we were considering. Here perhaps his thought is that "legal" implies "conventional" or "somehow fictitious" and hence that here there cannot be anything that needs the serious attention of a philosopher who is interested in existence.

Now it is on the face of it absurd to say that "A and B got married", "A gave B to C", "A swore an oath", and similar propositions, are not reports of physical facts, of physical (historical) events, things that have taken place in the overt, public history of the world. Nevertheless there is a deep inclination to say that in some sense it is true. We shall not get anywhere by simply pointing to the absurdity. But we might say: "All right: but in saying this you are showing part of what you mean by the expression 'physical fact'. A physical fact for you is one for which at least this holds: what a party to it thinks is indifferent. Thus when you say that these things are not physical facts, you are saying nothing substantial, but helping to fix the meaning of a term."

The accusation of absurdity could be met by a reformulation: "'A and B made a contract' is indeed the description of a physical event, but it is not a physical description of it, not a description in purely physical terms. And" – we might go on – "has not this already been conceded? For it was said that a set of conditions may hold, which are adequate for it to be true that a marriage is taking place except for this one point: that one of the parties does not think that what they are doing is getting married. Since it has been conceded that this marriage may fail to take place just because something is not thought, it is clear that 'A marriage has taken place' is a report in other than purely physical terms."

But the same point holds for 'description in purely physical terms' as I suggested for 'physical event': a description is defined as not being in purely physical terms by the fact that its holding is dependent on what is thought by the parties to the fact. Thus the physical is being partly defined negatively in terms of thought, and the statement that the making of a contract is not a merely physical fact is not a substantive inference from a contract's being made only if the parties think they are making a contract: it is a vaguer statement of that point.

What is true is that there are great areas of knowledge whose topics qualify to be called "physical" so far as this negative definition goes. The natural scientist is not concerned with facts which are formally dependent on human thought of them.

Let us now return to the first question: how is this possible? We have seen that it must be possible, that it must make sense to say that there are events such that their occurrence is formally dependent on the thought that they occur; but we have not seen how this is so.

We have the following situation about a type of concept. Let 'M' be a concept of such a type. Then (1) M-ings are events 'in the world', 'exterior' events: by this I mean that they are not just events in someone's soul. (2) When an M-ing takes place, someone, say A, M's. (3) If an M-ing takes place, in that A M's, it is an essential constituent of the M-ing that A thinks (believes) he is M-ing. Our problem was: what then is M-ing? For the explanation of it brings it in again as an unexplained term.

If a bottle is only a certain sort of bottle if it has a picture of itself on it, this seems to imply an infinite series of pictures and so A's thought that he is M-ing to involve an infinite series of thoughts. But that need not trouble us, if we say that to think something is also to think that you think it.

Our trouble lay in the impossibility of explaining the *content* of the thought, and in the consequent impossibility of saying what it is for an M-ing to take place, not in any implication that the content of the thought must in a way be conceived to be repeated *ad infinitum*. For about that we can say: All right, and what of it? "A thinks that . . ." does not mean that A actively performs a certain manoeuvre, so that he is in for performing an infinity of such manoeuvres if he performs one; in that sense, admittedly, he does not also think that he thinks, if he thinks. That is to say, if a certain thought *occurs* to him, it may or may not happen that another thought, namely the thought that the first thought occurs to him, also occurs to him; but we were not concerned with a thought occurring to someone, but with what he believes. So this was not our difficulty, though it is as well to mention it so as to put it aside.

But what is an M-ing if an M-ing is a state of affairs of which an essential constituent is the thought that it is an M-ing? To take a particular case, *what* is the making of a contract? This was Hume's first problem – he had two – lying behind his second one, which was: how is the *obligation* created? The first problem is not a problem about obligation; it exists for the concept prior to the generated obligation.

If the mistress of a man's passion is the mistress of his passion only because he loves her, there is no problem, because we can ask "Whom does he love, thereby making her the mistress of his passion?" and the answer mentions someone who exists whether or not she is the mistress of his passion, or if she does not he is in a state of illusion. But suppose there were such a thing as someone's having substantive existence because someone loved him. That seems impossible. Whom did the lover love, if he was not in a state of illusion? Something that characterizes an object as loved cannot be essential to its substantive description. Let us say that a state of affairs preceded by a description of it as an M given in a certain ceremonial manner is an M. The question arises: is there a description of states of affairs M not as Ms? Of course an object can be looked for, or its existence desired, before it exists, but if it then comes into existence, that which does come into existence must surely have a description independent of its being looked for, or desired to exist. And does not the same hold for thought as for love, desire or search? Even if my thinking can be a part cause of something's coming to be – which is often the case, since I bring things about by planning them and then carrying out the plan – all the same the thinking is only an efficient cause: the substantive fact that is caused partly by my thinking – assuming that what I plan is not itself a thought or set of thoughts, e.g. a calculation – can be described without mentioning what I think.

This, however, is precisely the thesis whose universality our counter-examples disprove. Making a contract is something that takes place only if it is thought by the parties that a contract is being made. A man may, indeed, not know in detail what the contract is, but if he could show that he was under the impression that he was, e.g., signing a quite different kind of document, such as a petition to the Queen, then he could claim not to have made the contract. More than this, a contract is made only if the parties intend to make a contract. For suppose someone in his ignorance thought that a contract could be made between him and another purely by some action on someone else's part, even though he himself should try with all his might to prevent the action and should never give his consent to the contract or empower the other to make a contract for him. Then he could think that a contract was being made, and the circumstances could be adequate for a contract to be made but for this one point, that he did not consent and had not previously empowered that other to act for him. Thus the thought, on the part of both supposedly contracting parties, that a contract is being made by a procedure (which does take place and) which could be a procedure of making a contract, does not secure that a contract is made. The will to make a

contract must be present in some form on the part of those between whom a
contract is made. Thus, e.g., a marriage is not a contract between husband
and wife if it is a contract between, say, husband and wife's father, such that,
once this contract has been made, the couple are married. In this case, of
course, the girl might be married without having any idea of the fact. It looks
as if the condition that the person who is getting married must think that he
is getting married, and the similar condition for all the concepts M which we
have considered, were based on the necessity for such things to be voluntary
to a higher or a lesser degree.

But what is a contract, or again, an undertaking? It is a sign whose
meaning is a contract or undertaking, voluntarily given as such. We are back
with our old problem. Let us try a new tack.

The contract contains a description of future proceedings; if the description does not turn out true, the contract or undertaking has not been kept or
at least not implemented. But this description is accompanied by a sign or
given in a form or manner which is what makes the whole a contract or undertaking and not, say, merely an expression of intention. What is the
meaning of the sign, supposing there is one? As Hume saw, it does not express an act of mind; we may hold – as I in fact do – that not even "I intend"
does that in Hume's sense; but for "I intend" it was more plausible to say it
did; for the sign of an undertaking or contract it is hopelessly implausible.
Now, let us imagine the *sign* of undertaking rather different from what we are
used to. Let it be the practice to have descriptions of the future sung in a
certain monotone, or written in green ink when they are undertakings, and
let this practice not be founded on an agreement – which would presuppose
that some expression for undertakings already existed – but be the expression for undertakings independent of any formulated agreement. In what
will it consist, that that monotone or that colour ink signify undertaking? Or
again: what will have given "you intoned it!" "you green inked it!" the force
of "you undertook . . ."?

This is Hume's problem. For the answer is: when something is written in
green ink, the man who wrote it is liable to be more restricted in what is (in
some sense of "possible") *possible* for him than he was before. That is to say,
writing it in green ink tends to produce some degree of, or some kind of,
necessity to do something which there was perhaps no necessity for him to do
before.

We must enquire into this sort of necessity and its correlative possibility.
For this sort of necessity will be, or be connected with, the necessity which is
usually called obligation.

The first thing we notice about this sort of necessity is that "necessarily p"
does not imply "p". Does it then imply "either p or q" where "q" expresses
some sort of undesirable consequences? We might put Hume's view in that
way: the man must do as he said *on pain of* never being trusted again. This
does not seem adequate, as in many cases all one incurs is the *danger* –
perhaps a fairly remote danger – of never being trusted again.

Aristotle in his dictionary says that in one sense of "necessary" the necessary is that without which good cannot be or come to be. (Of course the "cannot" in that sentence, as he later indicates, is not the negation of the possibility that is correlative with this sense of "necessary", but of the possibility that is correlative with absolute or "simple" necessity; for *this* it does hold that "necessarily p" implies "p".) He is evidently right; cf. "Is your journey really necessary?"

Shall we say, then, that when a man gives an undertaking he typically tends to restrict his (absolute) possibility of acting well, and so he typically tends to impose a (derivative) necessity on himself? Hume's problems will then assume the form: how can a sign *signify* such a restriction, just by being given, and how can one so use a mere sign to restrict one's possibility of acting well? We might be inclined to answer the latter: because it is bad to act unjustly, and breaking a contract that it was all right to make *is* acting unjustly. But that is not open to us when we are trying to explain what a contract is.

Certainly I cannot, just as I please, restrict my possibilities of good action by, say, inventing a sign "Bump!" and saying that the import of this is that when I attach it to a statement concerning my future actions it restricts my possibilities of acting well, thus: "Bump! I shall stand on my head! Now what I have done tends to bring it about that I do ill if I don't stand on my head, whereas without this it was quite open to me to stand on my head or not, without doing ill *qua* not standing on my head."

For one thing, an undertaking must be made to someone else. But even that is not enough. For if I go to someone and say "I undertake to stand on my head" and he replies: "But I don't want you to stand on your head", then I have not undertaken anything. An undertaking must be received by someone else and in someone's interest. The person who receives the undertaking and the person in whose interest it is made need not be the same; when they are not the same, the interest of the one must be a care of the other, whether by position or desire. It should also be said that "being in someone's interest" here *includes* "being in accord with his desire". Further, when the one who receives the undertaking is other than the one in whose interest it is made, then the one in whose interest is is made can be the one who gives the undertaking; otherwise not.

I should perhaps say here that I don't take an enormously strenuous view of the obligation created by the mere fact of having given an undertaking to do something. There are many cases of undertakings from the obligation of which a mere small degree of inconvenience exempts us. Sir W. D. Ross, when Pickard-Cambridge made some such point, replied that on receiving a promise people would want to know whether it was a Pickard-Cambridge sort of promise or the real sort! But I should say that people who are not maniacs know well enough, and that solemn commitments are comparative rarities, though they tend to be prominent when they occur.

Thus I say, not that giving an undertaking imposes a necessity, but that it *tends* to impose a necessity in that it *tends* to restrict the giver's possibilities of acting well. Further, this is not universal but only typical. For there is no doubt that I have given an undertaking if I have given an undertaking to do something wicked, or to do something not compossible with a prior strong contract; there is no doubt that two people can contract together to perform some evil action. But these undertakings or contracts impose no necessity to do the thing. (That does not mean that they can't be invoked at all: they can be invoked in demanding the return of money paid for an evil deed that was then not done.)

With so much ground cleared, we can come back to our main question. How can a sign, attached to a description of a future that is in someone's interest, tend to restrict my possibilities of doing well? The fact no longer seems so very paradoxical, when expressed in this form; but notice that the heart of the difficulty is still there. For the restriction is created, if it is created, purely by my voluntary giving of the sign. Suppose we say that the *meaning* of the sign is that my possibilities of doing well are restricted. But how can I make them be restricted in any way at all simply by saying that they are?

Returning to the suggested form "Bump! I will do so-and-so", let us ask how this could be learnt as an utterance having something of the same force as "I promise to do so-and-so". It will be characteristic that the learner is induced to say "Bump! I will . . ." and is then told "Now you've got to do it" and is then *made* to do the thing or reproached if he does not, and that the theme of the reproach is not merely that he did not do it after it was required of him, but that he failed to do it after saying "Bump! I will". He also learns to extract the utterance from others in connection with what he wants them to do and to use their having made it as a weapon in making them do what they have said they would, and as a ground of reproach if they do not. The one thing that gives "Bump" the significance of a promise is that the receiver .wants the thing to be done.

What I have sketched here is what Wittgenstein usefully and intelligibly called a "language-game", and we may say that it is a fact of nature that human beings very readily take to it. We can see at once that one whose "Bump" has been received *has* created *a* restriction for himself: namely on his possibilities of acting without danger of getting reproached, and pressed to act; and since it is inglorious to be reproached and annoying to be pressed, we can see that he has created for himself a reason for doing what he 'bumped' to do, when there is any danger of detection if he does not. But this is not yet to say that he has created a restriction either on his possibilities of doing well (as opposed to *faring* well) or on his possibilities of acting without *deserving* reproach. For the content of the reproach is simply 'you did not do what you bumped to do' and nothing has yet been said to show why this is a reproach he needs to take account of beyond the inconvenience attendant on incurring it. To show, that is, why this is a reproach of any more significance than "You eat your peas with your knife". One may "go along with" such a reproach to a high degree – "*mitschwingen*" as Wittgenstein called it – in both cases, because of one's training, so as to take account of one's "bumps" when no one knows whether one does or not, or avoid eating peas with a knife in all circumstances. But why not break the spell?

It is at this point that the utility of the imagined procedure comes into consideration. Nevertheless let us note that our first problem has been solved with the description of the "language-game". For it is clear that what you do is not a move in a game unless the game is being played and you are one of the players, acting as such in making the move. That involves that you are acquainted with the game and have an appropriate background, and also appropriate *expectations* and *calculations* in connection with, e.g., moving this piece from point A to point B. To have these is to think you are playing the game. That is to say, when we put our problem, "If to M includes thinking you are M-ing, what can M-ing be? for the account of it will include mention of it as the content of a thought and so no account of it can be given", we made a mistake in supposing that the explanation of the thought of M-ing must include an *account* (of M-ing) as something *contained* in the thought. Let M be marrying. If someone seriously thought he was only rehearsing, he would not afterwards *act* as if he thought he was married: if he did so, his plea that he "thought it was only a rehearsal" would not be heard.

We also have some light on the concept of an 'exterior' event or action. Hitherto we have said "it is not something that *just* goes on in the soul". Now we may say: When an event, or action, is exterior, then there is always *something* that happens, whose happening is not disproved by any evidence as to the thoughts of the people involved. Perhaps they did not get married, but they went through certain movements and uttered certain sounds; perhaps he did not *say* anything, but word-like noises did come out of his mouth. And so on.

Thus we can understand how there can be concepts M such that thinking you are M-ing is an essential constituent of M-ing, and also how the mere voluntary giving of a sign can restrict one in one's possibilities of acting without incurring reproach; and it remains to see how you are not merely running the danger of, but deserving reproach, if you do not do what you undertook, and how the restriction on the possibilities of acting *well* can arise from giving an undertaking.

It is at this point that I cease to use the notion of a language-game, since I should find further application of it useless and unintelligible. Unintelligible, because I can see no procedure to describe as a language-game, other than that of using the language of "desert", of "keeping" and "breaking" your "word", of "justice" and "injustice" in the contexts where someone has, e.g., attached a certain sign to a statement that he will do so-and-so. Unless, indeed, all we mean by saying that a language-game is played is that the things we are discussing are said. But in that case the notion is useless; a mere superfluous bit of jargon.

I said that the utility of the kind of procedure I imagined comes in at the point where the question of desert and of the restriction on the possibility of acting well arises. Let us now go into this.

What ways are there of getting human beings to do things? You can make a man fall over by pushing him; you cannot usefully make his hand write a letter or mix concrete by pushing; for in general if you have to push his hand in the right way, you might as well not use him at all. You can order him to do what you want, and if you have authority he will perhaps obey you. Again if you have power to hurt him or help him according as he disregards or obeys your orders, or if he loves you so as to accord with your requests, you have a way of getting him to do things. However, few people have authority over everyone they need to get to do things, and few people either have power to hurt or help others without damage to themselves or command affection from others to such an extent as to be able to get them to do the things they need others to do. Those who have extensive authority and power cannot exercise it to get all the other people to do the things that meet their mutual requirements. So, though physical force seems a more certain way of producing desired physical results than any other, and authority and power to hurt or help and sometimes affection too, more potent than the feeble procedure of such a language-game as the one with "Bump!" that I described, yet in default of the possibility or utility of exerting physical force, and of the possibility of exercising authority or power to hurt and help, or of commanding affection, this feeble means is at least *a* means of getting people to do things. Now getting one another to do things without the application of physical force is a necessity for human life, and that far beyond what could be secured by those other means.

Thus such a procedure as that language-game is an instrument whose use is part and parcel of an enormous amount of human activity and hence of human good; of the supplying both of human needs and of human wants so far as the satisfactions of these are compossible. It is scarcely possible to live in a society without encountering it and even actually being involved in it. Then not to 'go along with it', in the sense of accepting the necessity expressed by "Now you've got to . . ." after one has given the sign, will tend to hamper the attainment of the advantages that the procedure serves. It may be asked: "But what is this necessity?" The answer is given only by describing the procedure, the language-game, which as far as concerns the 'necessity' *expressed in it* does not differ from this one: "I say 'ping' and you have to say 'pong'". "You have to" has of course other uses, typically by someone powerful or authoritative who can make you do something. But if told "you have to say 'pong' when I say 'ping'", there is clearly no answer to "Why do I have to?" and so also initially with the language-game: "you have to do it if you say 'Bump! I'll do it'". But if the procedure has the role of an instrument in people's attainment of so many of the goods of common life, the necessity that people should both actually adopt the procedure, i.e. often give undertakings; and also go along with the procedure, i.e. tend to accept the necessity expressed in that reaction and also treat this as a *rule* – this necessity is a necessity of a quite different sort: it is the necessity that Aristotle spoke of, by which something is called necessary if without it good cannot be attained. And hence it comes about that by the voluntary giving of a sign I can restrict my possibilities of acting *well* and hence it can lead to my deserving, as well as receiving, reproach. This whole complex is, I believe, one of several roots of the idea of *justice*.

All this, it may be said, does not prove the *necessity* of acting justly in the matter of contracts; it only shows that a man will not act well – do what is good – if he does not do so. *That* necessity which is the first one to have the awful character of *obligation*, is a tabu or sacredness which is annexed to this sort of instrument of human good. It is like the sacredness of ambassadors and serves the same purpose.

Not even this, however, proves the necessity of respecting this tabu. If a man does not respect it, you may make it necessary for him to do so by the terror of the law; but that is not itself a recognition on his part. For that, there is needed the extra 'principle' as it is called, that it is necessary to act well, to do what is good, and avoid acting badly. If a man does not have this principle, then he may grant that to act unjustly is to act ill, but refuse to infer from this that it is necessary not to act unjustly. This, however, does not show that "it is necessary not to act unjustly" needs an extra *premise* if it is to be inferred from "to act unjustly is to act ill". For "necessary" here has that sense to which Aristotle draws attention, but now relates to the good of the agent not, as before, to the common good. Acting unjustly about contracts, you must be doing ill, if acting justly about them is a principal means by which human activities are promoted and human goods attained; but perhaps you think that you can attain your own good without acting well, and even if this is not true, it is not shown to be untrue by the considerations which show that acting unjustly is not acting well. For this reason it is intelligible for a man to say he sees no necessity to act well in that matter, that is, no necessity for himself to take contracts seriously except as it serves his purposes. But if someone does genuinely *take* a proof that without doing X he cannot act well as a proof that he must do X, then this shows, not that he has an extra premise, but that he *has a purpose* that can be served only by acting well, as such.

An analogy to illustrate this point: a doctor can take the fact that something possible is necessary for the cure of his patient's illness as showing straight off that he must prescribe it, without putting in the extra premise that it is necessary for him to prescribe such possible things as are necessary to cure illnesses of his patient. That is because he aims at the health of his patient. But if he aims at something else, such as knowledge, then he needs to be satisfied that it is necessary for him to prescribe what (being possible) is necessary to cure this illness, before the fact that this treatment is necessary for the cure will show him that he must prescribe it.

Thus "it is necessary to do what is good and avoid what is bad" is required as a premise only by someone with a purpose which can be served by acting ill. However, one constantly has such purposes. Then only a man for whom such purposes are subsidiary to a main purpose which cannot be so served will not need the principle; for him it will be nothing but a principle of inference, which is not a premise. Aristotle's conception of 'choice' is one according to which a man chooses to do only those actions which are governed by a main purpose; since he held – though surely he was wrong – that everyone has a main end such that if he acts purposively at all he acts for that end, he tried to make this concept of choice occupy the place in the analysis of action that ought to be occupied by the concept of intention. I used to think his idea of choice a mere misconception; but the above considerations have made me change my mind. Now even if not everyone has a main purpose there is such a thing as having one. It may be that in some sense everyone wishes for happiness; but that is not enough to make it true that everyone has a main purpose. For, firstly, what people wish for they do not necessarily try to get, and secondly, if one is trying to get happiness this may consist in trying to get something the possession of which one believes will be happiness, and only in having such a substantive aim can one be said to have a main purpose. Or if one can simply try to get happiness in whatever way it looks as if it might come, so that happiness can itself be called one's substantive aim, then happiness is *not* necessarily what everyone aims at. But if there is some substantive aim the attainment of which is conceived to be, and really is, happiness, and if it is such that it obviously could not be attained but only hindered by acting ill, then someone who had that aim would need no step from the proof that doing X is acting ill to the conclusion that he must not do X. For here there is no room for the question "Granted this is acting ill, still may it not be necessary for me – i.e. be that without which I cannot attain my end?" Similarly if a man's main purpose were to *be moral*. But for other people who have no substantive main purpose, what is only a principle of inference for the man with a purpose that can't be served by acting ill appears rather as a principle in the sense of an *axiom*, the principle, that is, that it is necessary to do what is good and avoid what is bad. But this axiom is not capable of demonstration except as generally holding. That it generally holds is no surprise, since kinds of action are proved to be good or bad by their role in generally promoting or hampering people's good. It is the tight corner that presents the theoretical difficulty, but it is just in the tight corner that the strength of the axiom shows itself. This comes out in the deliberate shamelessness needed to say "so what?" to the consideration that such-and-such is a bad kind of action. Rather than do that, it is common to find some way of making out that after all it is not. Now the necessity of which the axiom speaks is that necessity of that without which good cannot come about to which Aristotle drew our attention. Thus a man who has a main purpose different from one for the attainment of which doing what is good and avoiding what is bad is an *essential* means will not have the principle as an axiom, nor yet of course as a principle of inference: when he employs it at all it will be because he has satisfied himself that in this case his main purpose cannot be attained without doing what is good or avoiding what is bad. Much as if the doctor whose object was knowledge satisfied himself that in this case knowledge could not be attained without trying to cure the patient. But those whose reactions show that for them the principle operates as an *axiom* appear either to be making morality itself their substantive aim, testifying that there is a substantive good, even though they do not know what it is, or at any rate do not make that their good which nevertheless is their good, and for whose attainment doing what is good and avoiding what is bad is an essential means.

3   On Brute Facts

Following Hume I might say to my grocer: "Truth consists in agreement either to relations of ideas, as that twenty shillings make a pound, or to matters of fact, as that you have delivered me a quarter of potatoes; from this you can see that the term does not apply to such a proposition as that I owe you so much for the potatoes. You really must not jump from an 'is' – as, that it really is the case that I asked for the potatoes and that you delivered them and sent me a bill – to an 'owes'."

Does my owing the grocer in this case consist in any facts beyond the ones mentioned? No. Someone may want to say: it consists in these facts in the context of our institutions. This is correct in a way. But we must be careful, so to speak, to bracket that analysis correctly. That is, we must say, not: It consists in these-facts-holding-in-the-context-of-our-institutions, but: It consists in these facts – in the context of our institutions, or: In the context of our institutions it consists in these facts. For the statement that I owe the grocer does not contain a description of our institutions, any more than the statement that I gave someone a shilling contains a description of the institution of money and of the currency of this country. On the other hand, it requires these or very similar institutions as background in order so much as to be the *kind* of statement that it is.

Given this background, these facts do not necessarily amount to my owing the grocer such-and-such a sum. For the transaction might have been arranged as part of an amateur film production. Then perhaps I have said to the grocer "Send so many potatoes" and he has sent them, and he has sent a bill – but the whole procedure was not a real sale but a piece of acting; even though it so happens that I then eat the potatoes (not as part of the film): for perhaps the grocer has said I can keep them; or has said nothing but doesn't care, and the question never comes up. Thus the fact that something is done in a society with certain institutions, in the context of which it ordinarily amounts to such-and-such a transaction, is not absolute proof that such-and-such a transaction has taken place.

It is *intention* that makes the difference? Not if we think of intention as purely interior. What is true is this: what ordinarily amounts to such-and-such a transaction *is* such-and-such a transaction, unless a special context gives it a different character. But we should not include among special contexts the circumstance that I am suddenly deprived of all my goods and put in prison (through no fault of my own, if you like) – so that I can't pay the grocer. For in those circumstances it is still true to say that I owe him money.

Nor is there ordinarily any need to look about for a special context so as to make sure there is none that makes a radical difference. Ordinarily there is not; or if there is it usually comes very readily to light, though not always: which is why it is true to say that deception is always possible. But it is not theoretically possible to make provision in advance for the exception of extraordinary cases; for one can theoretically always suppose a further special context for each special context, which puts *it* in a new light.

Let us return to the move of saying: "Owing the grocer consists in these facts, in the context of our institutions." We ought to notice that exactly the same holds for the facts themselves as we described them. A set of events is the ordering and supplying of potatoes, and something is a bill, only in the context of our institutions.

Now if my owing the grocer on this occasion does not consist in any facts beyond the facts mentioned, it seems that we must say one of two things. Either (1) to say I owe the grocer is nothing but to say that *some such* facts hold, or (2) to say I owe the grocer adds something non-factual to the statement that some such facts hold.

But of course, if this is a valid point, it holds equally for the description of a set of events as: the grocer's supplying me with potatoes. And we should not wish to say either of these things about that.

The grocer supplies me with a quarter of potatoes: that is to say, he (1) brings that amount of potatoes to my house and (2) leaves them there. But not any action of taking a lot of potatoes to my house and leaving them there would be *supplying* me with them. If, for example, by the grocer's own arrangement, someone else, who had nothing to do with me, came and took them away soon afterwards, the grocer could not be said to have supplied me. – *When*, one might ask, did he supply me? Obviously, when he left the potatoes; it would be absurd to add "and also when he did *not* send to take them away again".

There can be no such thing as an exhaustive description of *all* the circumstances which theoretically could impair the description of an action of leaving a quarter of potatoes in my house as "supplying me with a quarter of potatoes". If there were such an exhaustive description, one could say that "supplying me with a quarter of potatoes" *means* leaving them at my house, together with the absence of any of those circumstances. As things are, we could only say "It means leaving them . . . together with the absence of any of the circumstances which would impair the description of that action as an action of supplying me with potatoes"; which is hardly an explanation. But I can know perfectly well that the grocer has supplied me with potatoes; asked what this consisted in, I say there was nothing to it but that I had ordered them and he brought them to my house.

Every description presupposes a context of normal procedure, but that context is not even implicitly described by the description. Exceptional circumstances could always make a difference, but they do not come into consideration without reason.

As compared with supplying me with a quarter of potatoes we might call carting a quarter of potatoes to my house and leaving them there a "brute fact". But as compared with the fact that I owe the grocer such-and-such a sum of money, that he supplied me with a quarter of potatoes is itself a brute fact. In relation to many descriptions of events or states of affairs which are asserted to hold, we can ask what the 'brute facts' were; and this will mean the facts which held, and in virtue of which, in a proper context, such-and-such a description is true or false, and which are more 'brute' than the alleged fact answering to that description. I will not ask here whether there are any facts that are, so to speak, 'brute' in comparison with leaving a quarter of potatoes at my house. On the other hand, one could think of facts in relation to which my owing the grocer such-and-such a sum of money is 'brute' – e.g. the fact that I am solvent.

We can now state some of the relations which at least sometimes hold between a description, say A, and descriptions, say xyz, of facts which are brute in relation to the fact described by A.

(1) There is a *range* of sets of such descriptions xyz such that some set of the range must be true if the description A is to be true. But the range can only ever be roughly indicated, and the way to indicate it is by giving a few diverse examples.

(2) The existence of the description A in the language in which it occurs presupposes a context, which we will call "the institution behind A"; this context may or may not be presupposed to elements in the descriptions xyz. For example, the institution of buying and selling is presupposed to the description "sending a bill", as it is to "being owed for goods received", but not to the description "supplying potatoes".

(3) A is not a description of the institution behind A.

(4) If some set holds out of the range of sets of descriptions some of which must hold if A is to hold, and if the institution behind A exists, then 'in normal circumstances' A holds. The meaning of "in normal circumstances" can only be indicated roughly, by giving examples of exceptional circumstances in which A would not hold.

(5) To assert the truth of A is not to assert that the circumstances were 'normal'; but if one is asked to justify A, the truth of the description xyz is in normal circumstances an adequate justification: A is not verified by any further facts.

(6) If A entails some other description B, then xyz cannot generally be said to entail B, but xyz together with normality of circumstances relatively to such descriptions as A can be said to entail B. For example: "He supplied me with potatoes" entails "The potatoes came into my possession." Further, "He had the potatoes brought to my house and left there" is in normal circumstances an adequate justification for saying "He supplied me with potatoes"; asked what his action of supplying me with potatoes consisted in, one would normally have no further facts to mention. (One *cannot* mention all the things that were *not* the case, which would have made a difference if

they had been.) But "He had potatoes carted to my house and left there" does *not* entail "The potatoes came into my possession". On the other hand "He had potatoes carted to my house and left there and the circumstances were just the normal circumstances as far as concerns being supplied with goods" does entail "The potatoes came into my possession."

4 Modern Moral Philosophy

I will begin by stating three theses which I present in this paper. The first is that it is not profitable for us at present to do moral philosophy; that should be laid aside at any rate until we have an adequate philosophy of psychology, in which we are conspicuously lacking. The second is that the concepts of obligation, and duty – *moral* obligation and *moral* duty, that is to say – and of what is *morally* right and wrong, and of the *moral* sense of "ought", ought to be jettisoned if this is psychologically possible; because they are survivals, or derivatives from survivals, from an earlier conception of ethics which no longer generally survives, and are only harmful without it. My third thesis is that the differences between the well-known English writers on moral philosophy from Sidgwick to the present day are of little importance.

Anyone who has read Aristotle's *Ethics* and has also read modern moral philosophy must have been struck by the great contrasts between them. The concepts which are prominent among the moderns seem to be lacking, or at any rate buried or far in the background, in Aristotle. Most noticeably, the term "moral" itself, which we have by direct inheritance from Aristotle, just doesn't seem to fit, in its modern sense, into an account of Aristotelian ethics. Aristotle distinguishes virtues as moral and intellectual. Have some of what he calls "intellectual" virtues what *we* should call a "moral" aspect? It would seem so; the criterion is presumably that a failure in an 'intellectual' virtue – like that of having good judgement in calculating how to bring about something useful, say in municipal government – may be *blameworthy*. But – it may reasonably be asked – cannot *any* failure be made a matter of blame or reproach? Any derogatory criticism, say of the workmanship of a product or the design of a machine, can be called blame or reproach. So we want to put in the word "morally" again: sometimes such a failure may be *morally* blameworthy, sometimes not. Now has Aristotle got this idea of *moral* blame, as opposed to any other? If he has, why isn't it more central? There are some mistakes, he says, which are causes, not of involuntariness in actions, but of scoundrelism, and for which a man is blamed. Does this mean that there is a *moral* obligation not to make certain intellectual mistakes? Why doesn't he discuss obligation in general, and this obligation in particular? If someone professes to be expounding Aristotle and talks in a modern fashion about "moral" such-and-such, he must be very imperceptive if he does not constantly feel like someone whose jaws have somehow got out of alignment: the teeth don't come together in a proper bite.

We cannot, then, look to Aristotle for any elucidation of the modern way

From *Philosophy*, 33 (1958).

of talking about "moral" goodness, obligation, etc. And all the best-known writers on ethics in modern times, from Butler to Mill, appear to me to have faults as thinkers on the subject which make it impossible to hope for any direct light on it from them. I will state these objections with the brevity which their character makes possible.

Butler exalts conscience, but appears ignorant that a man's conscience may tell him to do the vilest things.

Hume defines "truth" in such a way as to exclude ethical judgements from it, and professes that he has proved that they are so excluded. He also implicitly defines "passion" in such a way that aiming at anything is having a passion. His objection to passing from "is" to "ought" would apply equally to passing from "is" to "owes" or from "is" to "needs". (However, because of the historical situation, he has a point here, which I shall return to.)

Kant introduces the idea of 'legislating for oneself', which is as absurd as if in these days, when majority votes command great respect, one were to call each reflective decision a man made a *vote* resulting in a majority, which as a matter of proportion is overwhelming, for it is always 1–0. The concept of legislation requires superior power in the legislator. His own rigoristic convictions on the subject of lying were so intense that it never occurred to him that a lie could be relevantly described as anything but just a lie (e.g. as "a lie in such-and-such circumstances"). His rule about universalizable maxims is useless without stipulations as to what shall count as a relevant description of an action with a view to constructing a maxim about it.

Bentham and Mill do not notice the difficulty of the concept 'pleasure'. They are often said to have gone wrong through committing the naturalistic fallacy; but this charge does not impress me, because I do not find accounts of it coherent. But the other point – about pleasure – seems to me a fatal objection from the very outset. The ancients found this concept pretty baffling. It reduced Aristotle to sheer babble about 'the bloom on the cheek of youth' because, for good reasons, he wanted to make it out both identical with and different from the pleasurable activity. Generations of modern philosophers found this concept quite unperplexing, and it reappeared in the literature as a problematic one only a year or two ago when Ryle wrote about it. The reason is simple: since Locke, pleasure was taken to be some sort of internal impression. But it was superficial, if that was the right account of it, to make it the point of actions. One might adapt something Wittgenstein said about 'meaning' and say "Pleasure cannot be an internal impression, for no internal impression could have the consequences of pleasure".

Mill also, like Kant, fails to realize the necessity for stipulation as to relevant descriptions, if his theory is to have content. It did not occur to him that acts of murder and theft could be otherwise described. He holds that where a proposed action is of such a kind as to fall under some one principle established on grounds of utility, one must go by that; where it falls under none or several, the several suggesting contrary views of the action, the thing to do is to calculate particular consequences. But pretty well any action can be so described as to make it fall under a variety of principles of utility (as I shall say for short) if it falls under any.

I will now return to Hume. The features of Hume's philosophy which I have mentioned, like many other features of it, would incline me to think that Hume was a mere – brilliant – sophist; and his procedures are certainly sophistical. But I am forced, not to reverse, but to add to, this judgement by a peculiarity of Hume's philosophizing: namely that, although he reaches his conclusions – with which he is in love – by sophistical methods, his considerations constantly open up very deep and important problems. It is often the case that in the act of exhibiting the sophistry one finds oneself noticing matters which deserve a lot of exploring: the obvious stands in need of investigation as a result of the points that Hume pretends to have made. In this, he is unlike, say, Butler. It was already well-known that conscience could dictate vile actions; for Butler to have written disregarding this does not open up any new topics for us. But with Hume it is otherwise: hence he is a very profound and great philosopher, in spite of his sophistry. For example:

Suppose that I say to my grocer "Truth consists in *either* relations of ideas, as that 20s. = £1, *or* matters of fact, as that I ordered potatoes, you supplied them, and you sent me a bill. So it doesn't apply to such a proposition as that I *owe* you such-and-such a sum."

Now if one makes this comparison, it comes to light that the relation of the facts mentioned to the description "X owes Y so much money" is an interesting one, which I will call that of being "brute relative to" that description. Further, the 'brute' facts mentioned here themselves have descriptions relatively to which *other* facts are 'brute' – as, e.g., *he had potatoes carted to my house* and *they were left there* are brute facts relative to "he supplied me with potatoes". And the fact *X owes Y money* is in turn 'brute' relative to other descriptions – e.g. "X is solvent." Now the relation of 'relative bruteness' is a complicated one. To mention a few points: if xyz is a set of facts brute relative to a description A, then xyz is a set out of a range some set among which holds if A holds; but the holding of some set among these does not necessarily entail A, because exceptional circumstances can always make a difference; and what are exceptional circumstances relatively to A can generally only be explained by giving a few diverse examples, and *no* theoretically adequate provision can be made for exceptional circumstances, since a further special context can theoretically always be imagined that would reinterpret any special context. Further, though in normal circumstances, xyz would be a justification for A, that is not to say that A just comes to the same as "xyz"; and also there is apt to be an institutional context which gives its point to the description A, of which institution A is of course not itself a description. (For example, the statement that I give someone a shilling is not a description of the institution of money or of the currency of this country.) Thus, though it would be ludicrous to pretend that there can be no such thing as a transition from, e.g., "is" to "owes", the character of the transition is in fact rather interesting and comes to light as a result of reflecting on Hume's arguments.[1]

That I owe the grocer such-and-such a sum would be one of a set of facts which would be 'brute' in relation to the description "I am a bilker." 'Bilking' is of course a species of 'dishonesty' or 'injustice'. (Naturally the consideration will not have any effect on my actions unless I want to commit or avoid acts of injustice.)

So far, in spite of their strong associations, I conceive 'bilking', 'injustice' and 'dishonesty' in a merely 'factual' way. That I can do this for 'bilking' is obvious enough; 'justice' I have no idea how to define, except that its sphere is that of actions which relate to someone else, but "injustice", for its defect, can provisionally be offered as a generic name covering various species, e.g. bilking, theft (which is relative to whatever property institutions exist), slander, adultery, punishment of the innocent.

In present-day philosophy an explanation is required how an unjust man is a bad man, or an unjust action a bad one; to give such an explanation belongs to ethics; but it cannot even be begun until we are equipped with a sound philosophy of psychology. For the proof that an unjust man is a bad man would require a positive account of justice as a 'virtue'. This part of the subject-matter of ethics is, however, completely closed to us until we have an account of what *type of characteristic* a virtue is – a problem, not of ethics, but of conceptual analysis – and how it relates to the actions in which it is instanced: a matter which I think Aristotle did not succeed in really making clear. For this we certainly need an account at least of what a human action is at all, and how its description as "doing such-and-such" is affected by its motive and by the intention or intentions in it; and for this an account of such concepts is required.

The terms "should" or "ought" or "needs" relate to good and bad: e.g. machinery needs oil, or should or ought to be oiled, in that running without oil is bad for it, or it runs badly without oil. According to this conception, of course, "should" and "ought" are not used in a special 'moral' sense when one says that a man should not bilk. (In Aristotle's sense of the term "moral" (ἠθικός), they are being used in connection with a *moral* subject-matter: namely that of human passions and (non-technical) actions.) But they have now acquired a special so-called 'moral' sense – i.e. a sense in which they imply some absolute verdict (like one of guilty / not guilty on a man) on what is described in the "ought" sentences used in certain types of context: not merely the contexts that *Aristotle* would call "moral" – passions and actions – but also some of the contexts that he would call "intellectual".

The ordinary (and quite indispensable) terms "should", "needs", "ought", "must" – acquired this special sense by being equated in the relevant contexts with "is obliged", or "is bound", or "is required to", in

---

[1] The above two paragraphs are an abstract of the paper "On Brute Facts", chapter 3 of this volume.

the sense in which one can be obliged or bound by law, or something can be required by law.

How did this come about? The answer is in history: between Aristotle and us came Christianity, with its *law* conception of ethics. For Christianity derived its ethical notions from the Torah. (One might be inclined to think that a law conception of ethics could arise only among people who accepted an allegedly divine positive law; that this is not so is shown by the example of the Stoics, who also thought that whatever was involved in conformity to human virtues was required by divine law.)

In consequence of the dominance of Christianity for many centuries, the concepts of being bound, permitted, or excused became deeply embedded in our language and thought. The Greek word "ἁμαρτάνειν", the aptest to be turned to that use, acquired the sense "sin", from having meant "mistake", "missing the mark", "going wrong". The Latin *peccatum* which roughly corresponded to ἁμάρτημα was even apter for the sense "sin", because it was already associated with "culpa" – "guilt" – a juridical term. The blanket term "illicit", "unlawful", meaning much the same as our blanket term "wrong", explains itself. It is interesting that Aristotle did not have such a blanket term. He has blanket terms for wickedness – "villain", "scoundrel"; but of course a man is not a villain or a scoundrel by the performance of one bad action, or a few bad actions. And he has terms like "disgraceful", "impious"; and specific terms signifying defect of the relevant virtue, like "unjust"; but no term corresponding to "illicit". The extension of this term (i.e. the range of its application) could be indicated in his terminology only by a quite lengthy sentence: that is 'illicit' which, whether it is a thought or a consented-to passion or an action or an omission in thought or action, is something contrary to one of the virtues the lack of which shows a man to be bad *qua* man. That formulation would yield a concept coextensive with the concept 'illicit'.

To have a *law* conception of ethics is to hold that what is needed for conformity with the virtues failure in which is the mark of being bad *qua* man (and not merely, say *qua* craftsman or logician) – that what is needed for *this*, is required by divine law. Naturally it is not possible to have such a conception unless you believe in God as a law-giver; like Jews, Stoics and Christians. But if such a conception is dominant for many centuries, and then is given up, it is a natural result that the concepts of 'obligation', of being bound or required as by a law, should remain though they had lost their root; and if the word "ought" has become invested in certain contexts with the sense of "obligation", it too will remain to be spoken with a special emphasis and a special feeling in these contexts.

It is as if the notion 'criminal' were to remain when criminal law and criminal courts had been abolished and forgotten. A Hume discovering this situation might conclude that there was a special sentiment, expressed by "criminal", which alone gave the word its sense. So Hume discovered the situation in which the notion 'obligation' survived, and the word "ought" was invested with that peculiar force having which it is said to be used in a 'moral' sense, but in which the belief in divine law had long since been abandoned: for it was substantially given up among Protestants at the time of the Reformation.[2] The situation, if I am right, was the interesting one of the survival of a concept outside the framework of thought that made it a really intelligible one.

When Hume produced his famous remarks about the transition from "is" to "ought", he was, then, bringing together several quite different points. One I have tried to bring out by my remarks on the transition from "is" to "owes" and on the relative 'bruteness' of facts. It would be possible to bring out a different point by enquiring about the transition from "is" to "needs"; from the characteristics of an organism to the environment that it needs, for example. To say that it needs that environment is not to say, e.g., that you want it to have that environment, but that it won't flourish unless it has it. Certainly, it all depends whether you *want* it to flourish! as Hume would say. But what 'all depends' on whether you want it to flourish is whether the fact that it needs that environment, or won't flourish without it, has the slightest influence on your actions. Now *that* such-and-such 'ought' to be or 'is needed' is supposed to have an influence on your actions: from which it seemed natural to infer that to judge that it 'ought to be' was in fact to grant what you judged 'ought to be' influence on your actions. And no amount of truth as to what *is* the case could possibly have a logical claim to have influence on your actions. (It is not judgement as such that sets us in motion; but our judgement on how to get or do something we *want*.) Hence it *must* be impossible to infer "needs" or "ought to be" from "is". But in the case of a plant, let us say, the inference from "is" to "needs" is certainly not in the least dubious. It is interesting and worth examining; but not at all fishy. Its interest is similar to the interest of the relation between brute and less brute facts: these relations have been very little considered. And while you can contrast 'what it needs' with 'what it's got' – like contrasting *de facto* and *de iure* – that does not make its needing this environment less of a 'truth'.

Certainly in the case of what the plant needs, the thought of a need will only affect action if you want the plant to flourish. Here, then, there is no necessary connection between what you can judge the plant 'needs' and what you want. But there is some sort of necessary connection between what you think *you* need, and what you want. The connection is a complicated one; it is possible *not* to want something that you judge you need. But, e.g., it is not possible never to want *anything* that you judge you need. This, however, is not a fact about the meaning of the word "to need", but about the phenomenon of *wanting*. Hume's reasoning, we might say, in effect, leads one to think it must be about the word "to need", or "to be good for".

[2] They did not deny the existence of divine law; but their most characteristic doctrine was that it was given, not to be obeyed, but to show man's incapacity to obey it, even by grace; and this applied not merely to the ramified prescriptions of the Torah, but to the requirements of 'natural divine law'. Cf. in this connection the decree of Trent against the teaching that Christ was only to be trusted in as mediator, not obeyed as legislator.

Thus we find two problems already wrapped up in the remark about a transition from "is" to "ought"; now supposing that we had clarified the 'relative bruteness' of facts on the one hand, and the notions involved in 'needing', and 'flourishing' on the other – there would *still* remain a third point. For, following Hume, someone might say: Perhaps you have made out your point about a transition from "is" to "owes" and from "is" to "needs": but only at the cost of showing "owes" and "needs" sentences to express a *kind* of truths, a *kind* of facts. And it remains impossible to infer *"morally ought"* from "is".

This comment, it seems to me, would be correct. This word "ought", having become a word of mere mesmeric force, could not, in the character of having that force, be inferred from anything whatever. It may be objected that it could be inferred from other "morally ought" sentences: but that cannot be true. The appearance that this is so is produced by the fact that we say "All men are φ" and "Socrates is a man" implies "Socrates is φ". But here "φ" is a dummy predicate. We mean that if you substitute a real predicate for "φ" the implication is valid. A real predicate is required; not just a word containing no intelligible thought: a word retaining the suggestion of force, and apt to have a strong psychological effect, but which no longer signifies a real concept at all.

For its suggestion is one of a *verdict* on my action, according as it agrees or disagrees with the description in the "ought" sentence. And where one does not think there is a judge or a law, the notion of a verdict may retain its psychological effect, but not its meaning. Now imagine that just this word "verdict" *were* so used – with a characteristically solemn emphasis – as to retain its atmosphere but not its meaning, and someone were to say: "For a *verdict*, after all, you need a law and a judge". The reply might be made: "Not at all, for if there were a law and a judge who gave a verdict, the question for us would be whether accepting that verdict is something that there is a *Verdict* on". This is an analogue of an argument which is so frequently referred to as decisive: If someone does have a divine law conception of ethics, all the same, he has to agree that he has to have a judgement that he *ought* (morally ought) to obey the divine law; so his ethic is in exactly the same position as any other: he merely has a 'practical major premise'[3]: "Divine law ought to be obeyed" where someone else has, e.g., "The greatest happiness principle ought to be employed in all decisions".

I should judge that Hume and our present-day ethicists had done a considerable service by showing that no content could be found in the notion "morally ought"; if it were not that the latter philosophers try to find an alternative (very fishy) content and to retain the psychological force of the term. It would be most reasonable to drop it. It has no reasonable sense outside a law conception of ethics; they are not going to maintain such a conception; and you can do ethics without it, as is shown by the example of

[3] As it is absurdly called. Since major premise=premise containing the term which is predicate in the conclusion, it is a solecism to speak of it in the connection with practical reasoning.

Aristotle. It would be a great improvement if, instead of "morally wrong", one always named a genus such as "untruthful", "unchaste", "unjust". We should no longer ask whether doing something was "wrong", passing directly from some description of an action to this notion; we should ask whether, e.g., it was unjust; and the answer would sometimes be clear at once.

I now come to the epoch in modern English moral philosophy marked by Sidgwick. There is a startling change that seems to have taken place between Mill and Moore. Mill assumes, as we saw, that there is no question of calculating particular consequences of an action such as murder or theft; and we saw too that his position was stupid, because it is not at all clear how an action *can* fall under just one principle of utility. In Moore and in subsequent academic moralists of England we find it taken to be pretty obvious that "the right action" means the one which produces the best possible consequences (reckoning among consequences the intrinsic values ascribed to certain kinds of act by some 'Objectivists'[4]). Now it follows from this that a man does well, subjectively speaking, if he acts for the best in the particular circumstances according to his judgement of the total consequences of this particular action. I say that this follows, not that any philosopher has said precisely that. For discussion of these questions can of course get extremely complicated: e.g. it can be doubted whether "such-and-such is the right action" is a satisfactory formulation, on the grounds that things have to exist to have predicates – so perhaps the best formulation is "I am obliged"; or again, a philosopher may deny that "right" is a 'descriptive' term, and then take a roundabout route through linguistic analysis to reach a view which comes to the same thing as "the right action is the one productive of the best consequences" (e.g. the view that you frame your 'principles' to effect the end you choose to pursue, the connection between "choice" and "best" being supposedly such that choosing reflectively means that you choose how to act so as to produce the best consequences); further, the roles of what are called "moral principles" and of the 'motive of duty' have to be described; the differences between "good" and "morally good" and "right" need to be explored, the special characteristics of "ought" sentences investigated. Such discussions generate an appearance of significant diversity of views where what is really significant is an overall similarity. The overall similarity is made clear if you consider that every one of the best known English academic moral philosophers has put out a philosophy according to which, e.g., it is not possible to hold that it cannot be right to kill the innocent as a means to any end whatsoever and that someone who thinks otherwise is in error. (I have to mention both points; because Mr Hare, for example, while teaching a philosophy which would encourage a person to judge that killing

---

[4] Oxford Objectivists of course distinguish between 'consequences' and 'intrinsic values' and so produce a misleading appearance of not being consequentialists. But they do not hold – and Ross explicitly denies – that the gravity of, e.g., procuring the condemnation of the innocent is such that it cannot be outweighed by, e.g., national interest. Hence their distinction is of no importance.

the innocent would be what he ought to choose for over-riding purposes, would also teach, I think, that if a man chooses to make avoiding killing the innocent for any purpose his 'supreme practical principle', he cannot be impugned for error: that just is his 'principle'. But with that qualification, I think it can be seen that the point I have mentioned holds good of every single English academic moral philosopher since Sidgwick.) Now this is a significant thing: for it means that all these philosophies are quite incompatible with the Hebrew–Christian ethic. For it has been characteristic of that ethic to teach that there are certain things forbidden whatever *consequences* threaten, such as: choosing to kill the innocent for any purpose, however good; vicarious punishment; treachery (by which I mean obtaining a man's confidence in a grave matter by promises of trustworthy friendship and then betraying him to his enemies); idolatry; sodomy; adultery; making a false profession of faith. The prohibition of certain things simply in virtue of their description as such-and-such identifiable kinds of action, regardless of any further consequences, is certainly not the whole of the Hebrew–Christian ethic; but it is a noteworthy feature of it; and, if every academic philosopher since Sidgwick has written in such a way as to exclude this ethic, it would argue a certain provinciality of mind not to see this incompatability as the most important fact about these philosophers, and the differences between them as somewhat trifling by comparison.

It is noticeable that none of these philosophers displays any consciousness that there is such an ethic, which he is contradicting: it is pretty well taken for obvious among them all that a prohibition such as that on murder does not operate in face of some consequences. But of course the strictness of the prohibition has as its point *that you are not to be tempted by fear or hope of consequences.*

If you notice the transition from Mill to Moore, you will suspect that it was made somewhere by someone; Sidgwick will come to mind as a likely name; and you will in fact find it going on, almost casually, in him. He is rather a dull author; and the important things in him occur in asides and footnotes and small bits of argument which are not concerned with his grand classification of the 'methods of ethics'. A divine law theory of ethics is reduced to an insignificant variety by a footnote telling us that "the best theologians" (God knows whom he meant) tell us that God is to be obeyed in his capacity of a *moral* being. ἤ φορτικός ὁ ἔπαινος; one seems to hear Aristotle saying: "Isn't the praise vulgar?" (*Eth. Nic.*, 1178b16) – But Sidgwick *is* vulgar in that kind of way: he thinks, for example, that humility consists in underestimating your own merits – i.e. in a species of untruthfulness; and that the ground for having laws against blasphemy was that it was offensive to believers; and that to go accurately into the virtue of purity is to offend against its canons, a thing he reproves "medieval theologians" for not realizing.

From the point of view of the present enquiry, the most important thing about Sidgwick was his definition of intention. He defines intention in such a way that one must be said to intend any foreseen consequences of one's voluntary action. This definition is obviously incorrect, and I dare say that no one would be found to defend it now. He uses it to put forward an ethical thesis which would now be accepted by many people: the thesis that it does not make any difference to a man's responsibility for something that he foresaw, that he felt no desire for it, either as an end or as a means to an end. Using the language of intention more correctly, and avoiding Sidgwick's faulty conception, we may state the thesis thus: it does not make any difference to a man's responsibility for an effect of his action which he can foresee, that he does not intend it. Now this sounds rather edifying; it is I think quite characteristic of very bad degenerations of thought on such questions that they sound edifying. We can see what it amounts to by considering an example. Let us suppose that a man has a responsibility for the maintenance of some child. Therefore deliberately to withdraw support from it is a bad sort of thing for him to do. It would be bad for him to withdraw its maintenance because he didn't want to maintain it any longer; *and* also bad for him to withdraw it because by doing so he would, let us say, compel someone else to do something. (We may suppose for the sake of argument that compelling that person to do that thing is in itself quite admirable.) But now he has to choose between doing something disgraceful and going to prison; if he goes to prison, it will follow that he withdraws support from the child. By Sidgwick's doctrine, there is no difference in his responsibility for ceasing to maintain the child, between the case where he does it for its own sake or as a means to some other purpose, and when it happens as a foreseen and unavoidable consequence of his going to prison rather than do something disgraceful. It follows that he must weigh up the relative badness of withdrawing support from the child and of doing the disgraceful thing; and it may easily be that the disgraceful thing is in fact a less vicious action than intentionally withdrawing support from the child would be; if then the fact that withdrawing support from the child is a side effect of his going to prison does not make any difference to his responsibility, this consideration will incline him to do the disgraceful thing; which can still be pretty bad. And of course, once he has started to look at the matter in this light, the only reasonable thing for him to consider will be the consequences and not the intrinsic badness of this or that action. So that, given that he judges reasonably that no *great* harm will come of it, he can do a much more disgraceful thing than deliberately withdrawing support from the child. And if his calculations turn out in fact wrong, it will appear that he was not responsible for the consequences, because he did not foresee them. For in fact Sidgwick's thesis leads to its being quite impossible to estimate the badness of an action except in the light of *expected* consequences. But if so, then *you* must estimate the badness in the light of the consequences *you* expect; and so it will follow that you can exculpate yourself from the *actual* consequences of the most discraceful actions, so long as you can make out a case for not having foreseen them. Whereas I should contend that a man is responsible for the bad consequences of his bad actions, but gets no credit for the good ones; and contrariwise is not responsible for the bad consequences of good actions.

The denial of *any* distinction between foreseen and intended consequences, as far as responsibility is concerned, was not made by Sidgwick in developing any one 'method of ethics'; he made this important move on behalf of everybody and just on its own account; and I think it plausible to suggest that *this* move on the part of Sidgwick explains the difference between old-fashioned Utilitarianism and that *consequentialism*, as I name it, which marks him and every English academic moral philosopher since him. By it, the kind of consideration which would formerly have been regarded as a temptation, the kind of consideration urged upon men by wives and flattering friends, was given a status by moral philosophers in their theories.

It is a necessary feature of consequentialism that it is a shallow philosophy. For there are always borderline cases in ethics. Now if you are either an Aristotelian, or a believer in divine law, you will deal with a borderline case by considering whether doing such-and-such in such-and-such circumstances is, say, murder, or is an act of injustice; and according as you decide it is or it isn't, you judge it to be a thing to do or not. This would be the method of casuistry; and while it may lead you to stretch a point on the circumference, it will not permit you to destroy the centre. But if you are a consequentialist, the question "What is it right to do in such-and-such circumstances?" is a stupid one to raise. The casuist raises such a question only to ask "Would it be *permissible* to do so-and-so?" or "Would it be permissible *not* to do so-and-so?" Only if it would *not* be permissible *not* to do so-and-so could he say "*This* would be *the* thing to do".[5] Otherwise, though he may speak *against* some action, he cannot prescribe any – for in an *actual* case, the circumstances (beyond the ones imagined) might suggest all sorts of possibilities, and you can't know in advance what the possibilities are going to be. Now the consequentialist has no footing on which to say "This would be permissible, this not"; because by his own hypothesis, it is the consequences that are to decide, and he has no business to pretend that he can lay it down what possible twists a man could give doing this or that; the most he can say is: a man must not *bring about* this or that; he has no right to say he will, in an actual case, bring about such-and-such unless he does so-and-so. Further, the consequentialist, in order to be imagining borderline cases at all, has of course to assume some sort of law or standard according to which this is a borderline case. Where then does he get the standard from? In practice the answer invariably is: from the standards current in his society or his circle. And it has in fact been the mark of all these philosophers that they have been extremely conventional; they have nothing in them by which to revolt against the conventional standards of their sort of people; it is impossible that they should be profound. But the chance that a whole range of

---

[5] Necessarily a rare case: for the positive precepts, e.g. "Honour your parents", hardly ever prescribe, and seldom even necessitate, any particular action.

conventional standards will be decent is small. Finally, the point of considering hypothetical situations, perhaps very improbable ones, *seems* to be to elicit from yourself or someone else a hypothetical decision to do something of a bad kind. I don't doubt this has the effect of predisposing people – who will never get into the situations for which they have made hypothetical choices – to consent to similar bad actions, or to praise and flatter those who do them, so long as their crowd does so too, when the desperate circumstances imagined don't hold at all.

Those who recognize the origins of the notions of 'obligation' and of the emphatic, 'moral', *ought*, in the divine law conception of ethics, but who reject the notion of a divine legislator, sometimes look about for the possibility of retaining a law conception without a divine legislator. This search, I think, has some interest in it. Perhaps the first thing that suggests itself is the 'norms' of a society. But just as one cannot be impressed by Butler when one reflects what conscience can tell people to do, so, I think, one cannot be impressed by this idea if one reflects what the 'norms' of a society can be like. That legislation can be 'for oneself' I reject as absurd; whatever you do 'for yourself' may be admirable; but is not legislating. Once one sees this, one may say: I have to frame my own rules, and these are the best I can frame, and I shall go by them until I know something better: as a man might say "I shall go by the customs of my ancestors". Whether this leads to good or evil will depend on the *content* of the rules or of the customs of one's ancestors. If one is lucky it will lead to good. Such an attitude would be hopeful in this at any rate: it seems to have in it some Socratic doubt where, from having to fall back on such expedients, it should be clear that Socratic doubt is good; in fact rather generally it must be good for anyone to think "Perhaps in some way I can't see, I may be on a bad path, perhaps I am hopelessly wrong in some essential way." The search for 'norms' might lead someone to look for laws of nature, as if the universe were a legislator; but in the present day this is not likely to lead to good results: it might lead one to eat the weaker according to the laws of nature, but would hardly lead anyone nowadays to notions of justice; the pre-Socratic feeling about justice as comparable to the balance or harmony which kept things going is very remote to us.

There is another possibility here: 'obligation' may be contractual. Just as we look at the law to find out what a man subject to it is required by it to do, so we look at a contract to find out what the man who has made it is required by it to do. Thinkers, admittedly remote from us, might have the idea of a *foedus rerum*, of the universe not as a legislator but as the embodiment of a contract. Then if you could find out what the contract was, you would learn your obligations under it. Now, you cannot be under a law unless it has been promulgated to you; and the thinkers who believed in 'natural divine law' held that it was promulgated to every grown man in his knowledge of good and evil. Similarly you cannot be in a contract without having contracted, i.e. given signs of entering upon the contract. Just possibly, it might be argued that the use of language which one makes in the ordinary conduct of life amounts in some sense to giving the signs of entering into various contracts. If anyone had this theory, we should want to see it worked out. I suspect that it would be largely formal; it might be possible to construct a system embodying the law (whose status might be compared to that of 'laws' of logic): "what's sauce for the goose is sauce for the gander," but hardly one descending to such particularities as the prohibition on murder or sodomy. Also, while it is clear that you can be subject to a law that you do not acknowledge and have not thought of as law, it does not seem reasonable to say that you can enter upon a contract without knowing that you are doing so; such ignorance is usually held to be destructive of the nature of a contract.

It might remain to look for 'norms' in human virtues: just as *man* has so many teeth, which is certainly not the average number of teeth men have, but is the number of teeth for the species, so perhaps the species *man*, regarded not just biologically, but from the point of view of the activity of thought and choice in regard to the various departments of life – powers and faculties and use of things needed – 'has' such-and-such virtues: and this 'man' with the complete set of virtues is the 'norm', as 'man' with, e.g., a complete set of teeth is a norm. But in *this* sense "norm" has ceased to be roughly equivalent to "law". In *this* sense the notion of a 'norm' brings us nearer to an Aristotelian than a law conception of ethics. There is, I think, no harm in that; but if someone looked in this direction to give "norm" a sense, then he ought to recognize what has happened to the term "norm", which he wanted to mean "law – without bringing God in": it has ceased to mean "law" at all; and *so* the expressions "moral obligation", "the moral ought", and "duty" are best put on the Index, if he can manage it.

But meanwhile – is it not clear that there are several concepts that need investigating simply as part of the philosophy of psychology and – as I should recommend – *banishing ethics totally* from our minds? Namely – to begin with: 'action', 'intention', 'pleasure', 'wanting'. More will probably turn up if we start with these. Eventually it might be possible to advance to considering the concept of a virtue; with which, I suppose, we should be beginning some sort of a study of ethics.

I will end by describing the advantages of using the word "ought" in a non-emphatic fashion, and not in a special 'moral' sense; of discarding the term "wrong" in a 'moral' sense, and using such notions as 'unjust'.

It is possible, if one is allowed to proceed just by giving examples, to distinguish between the intrinsically unjust, and what is unjust given the circumstances. Seriously to get a man judicially punished for something which it can be clearly seen he has not done is intrinsically unjust. This might be done, of course, and often has been done, in all sorts of ways; by suborning false witnesses, by a rule of law by which something is 'deemed' to be the case which is admittedly not the case as a matter of fact, and by open insolence on the part of the judges and powerful people when they more or less openly say: "A fig for the fact that you did not do it; we mean to sentence you for it all the same." What is unjust given, e.g., normal circumstances is to deprive people of their ostensible property without legal procedure, not to pay debts, not to keep contracts and a host of other things of the kind. Now, the circumstances can clearly make a great deal of difference in estimating the justice or injustice of such procedures as these; and these circumstances may *sometimes* include expected consequences; for example, a man's claim to a bit of property can become a nullity when its seizure and use can avert some obvious disaster: as, e.g., if you could use a machine of his to produce an explosion in which it would be destroyed, but by means of which you could divert a flood or make a gap which a fire could not jump. Now this certainly does not mean that what would ordinarily be an act of injustice, but is not intrinsically unjust, can always be rendered just by a reasonable calculation of better consequences; far from it; but the problems that would be raised in an attempt to draw a boundary line (or boundary area) here are obviously complicated. And while there are certainly some general remarks which ought to be made here, and some boundaries that can be drawn, the decision on particular cases would for the most part be determined κατὰ τὸν ὀρθὸν λόγον – "according to what's reasonable" – e.g. that *such-and-such* a delay of payment of a *such-and-such* debt to a person *so* circumstanced, on the part of a person *so* circumstanced, would or would not be unjust, is really only to be decided "according to what's reasonable"; and for this there can *in principle* be no canon other than giving a few examples. That is to say, while it is because of a big gap in philosophy that we can give no general account of the concept of virtue and of the concept of justice, but have to proceed, using the concepts, only by giving examples; still there is an area where it is not because of any gap, but is in principle the case, that there is no account except by way of examples: and that is where the canon is "what's reasonable": which of course is *not* a canon.

That is all I wish to say about what is just in some circumstances, unjust in others; and about the way in which expected consequences can play a part in determining what is just. Returning to my example of the intrinsically unjust: if a procedure *is* one of judicially punishing a man for what he is clearly understood not to have done, there can be absolutely no argument about the description of this as unjust. No circumstances, and no expected consequences, which do *not* modify the description of the procedure as one of judicially punishing a man for what he is known not to have done can modify the description of it as unjust. Someone who attempted to dispute this would only be pretending not to know what "unjust" means: for this is a paradigm case of injustice.

And here we see the superiority of the term "unjust" over the terms "morally right" and "morally wrong". For in the context of English moral philosophy since Sidgwick it appears legitimate to discuss whether it *might* be 'morally right' in some circumstances to adopt that procedure; but it cannot be argued that the procedure would in any circumstances be just.

Now I am not able to do the philosophy involved – and I think that no one in the present situation of English philosophy *can* do the philosophy involved – but it is clear that a good man is a just man; and a just man is a man who habitually refuses to commit or participate in any unjust actions for fear of any consequences, or to obtain any advantage, for himself or anyone else. Perhaps no one will disagree. But, it will be said, what *is* unjust is sometimes determined by expected consequences; and certainly that is true. But there are cases where it is not: now if someone says, "I agree, but all this wants a lot of explaining," then he is right, and, what is more, the situation at present is that we can't do the explaining; we lack the philosophic equipment. But if someone really thinks, *in advance*,[6] that it is open to question whether such an action as procuring the judicial execution of the innocent should be quite excluded from consideration – I do not want to argue with him; he shows a corrupt mind.

In such cases our moral philosophers seek to impose a dilemma upon us. "If we have a case where the term 'unjust' applies purely in virtue of a factual description, can't one raise the question whether one sometimes conceivably ought to do injustice? If 'what is unjust' is determined by consideration of whether it is *right* to do so-and-so in such-and-such circumstances, then the question whether it is 'right' to commit injustice can't arise, just because 'wrong' has been built into the definition of injustice. But if we have a case where the description 'unjust' applies purely in virtue of the facts, without bringing 'wrong' in, then the question can arise whether one 'ought' perhaps to commit an injustice, whether it might not be 'right' to. And of course 'ought' and 'right' are being used in their *moral* senses here. Now either you must decide what is 'morally right' in the light of certain *other* 'principles', or you make a 'principle' about *this* and decide that an injustice is never 'right'; but even if you do the latter you are going beyond the facts; you are making a decision that you will not, or that it is wrong to, commit injustice. But in either case, *if* the term 'unjust' is determined simply by the facts, it is not the term 'unjust' that determines that the term 'wrong' applies, but a decision that injustice is *wrong*, together with the diagnosis of the 'factual' description as entailing injustice. But the man who makes an absolute decision that injustice is 'wrong' has no footing on which to criticize someone who does *not* make that decision as judging falsely."

In this argument "wrong" of course is explained as meaning "morally wrong", and all the atmosphere of the term is retained while its substance is

---

[6] If he thinks it in the concrete situation, he is of course merely a normally tempted human being. In discussion when this paper was read, as was perhaps to be expected, this case was produced: a government is required to have an innocent man tried, sentenced and executed under threat of a 'hydrogen bomb war'. It would seem strange to me to have much hope of so averting a war threatened by such men as made this demand. But the most important thing about the way in which cases like this are invented in discussions, is the assumption that only two courses are open: here, compliance and open defiance. No one can say in advance of such a situation what the possibilities are going to be – e.g. that there is none of stalling by a feigned willingness to comply, accompanied by a skilfully arranged 'escape' of the victim.

guaranteed quite null. Now let us remember that "morally wrong" is the term which is the heir of the notion 'illicit', or 'what there is an obligation *not* to do'; which belongs in a divine law theory of ethics. Here it really does add something to the description "unjust" to say there is an obligation not to do it; for what obliges is the divine law – as rules oblige in a game. So if the divine law obliges not to commit injustice by forbidding injustice, it really does add something to the description "unjust" to say there is an obligation not to do it. And it is because 'morally wrong' is the heir of this concept, but an heir that is cut off from the family of concepts from which it sprang, that "morally wrong" *both* goes beyond the mere factual description "unjust" *and* seems to have no discernible content except a certain compelling force, which I should call purely psychological. And such is the force of the term that philosophers actually suppose that the divine law notion can be dismissed as making no essential difference even if it is held – *because* they think that a 'practical principle' running "I *ought* (i.e. am morally obliged) to obey divine laws" is required for the man who believes in divine laws. But actually this notion of obligation is a notion which only operates in the context of law. And I should be inclined to congratulate the present-day moral philosophers on depriving "morally ought" of its now delusive appearance of content, if only they did not manifest a detestable desire to retain the atmosphere of the term.

It may be possible, if we are resolute, to discard the term "morally ought", and simply return to the ordinary "ought", which, we ought to notice, is such an extremely frequent term of human language that it is difficult to imagine getting on without it. Now if we do return to it, can't it reasonably be asked whether one might ever need to commit injustice, or whether it won't be the best thing to do? Of course it can. And the answers will be various. One man – a philosopher – may say that since justice is a virtue, and injustice a vice, and virtues and vices are built up by the performances of the action in which they are instanced, an act of injustice will tend to make a man bad; and essentially the flourishing of a man *qua* man consists in his being good (e.g. in virtues); but for any X to which such terms apply, X needs what makes it flourish, so a man needs, or ought to perform, only virtuous actions; and even if, as it must be admitted may happen, he flourishes less, or not at all, in inessentials, by avoiding injustice, his life is spoiled in essentials by not avoiding injustice – so he still needs to perform only just actions. That is roughly how Plato and Aristotle talk; but it can be seen that philosophically there is a huge gap, at present unfillable as far as we are concerned, which needs to be filled by an account of human nature, human action, the type of characteristic a virtue is, and above all of human 'flourishing'. And it is the last concept that appears the most doubtful. For it is a bit much to swallow that a man in pain and hunger and poor and friendless is flourishing, as Aristotle himself admitted. Further, someone might say that one at least needed to stay alive to flourish. Another man unimpressed by all that will say in a hard case "What we need is such-and-such, which we won't get without doing this (which is unjust) – so this is what we ought to do". Another man, who does not follow the rather elaborate reasoning of the philosophers, simply says "I know it is in any case a disgraceful thing to say that one had better commit this unjust action." The man who believes in divine laws will say perhaps "It is forbidden, and however it looks, it cannot be to anyone's profit to commit injustice"; he like the Greek philosophers can think in terms of flourishing. If he is a Stoic, he is apt to have a decidedly strained notion of what flourishing consists in; if he is a Jew or Christian, he need not have any very distinct notion: the way it will profit him to abstain from injustice is something that he leaves it to God to determine, himself only saying "It can't do me any good to go against his law". (He also hopes for a great reward in a new life later on, e.g. at the coming of Messiah; but in this he is relying on special promises.)

It is left to modern moral philosophy – the moral philosophy of all the well-known English ethicists since Sidgwick – to construct systems according to which the man who says "We need such-and-such, and will only get it this way" *may* be a virtuous character: that is to say, it is left open to debate whether such a procedure as the judicial punishment of the innocent may not in some circumstances be the 'right' one to adopt; and though the present Oxford moral philosophers would accord a man *permission* to 'make it his principle' not to do such a thing, they teach a philosophy according to which the particular consequences of such an action *could* 'morally' be taken into account by a man who was debating what to do; and if they were such as to accord with his ends, it might be a step in his moral education to frame a moral principle under which he "managed" (to use Mr Nowell-Smith's phrase)[7] to bring the action; or it might be a new 'decision of principle', making which was an advance in the formation of his moral thinking (to adopt Mr Hare's conception), to decide: in such-and-such circumstances one ought to procure the judicial condemnation of the innocent. And that is my complaint.

---

[7] *Ethics*, (Harmondsworth, 1954), p. 308.

5   Authority in Morals

To many, at least of those who study philosophy, there are difficulties about any notion of authority in morals. There are, of course, various forms of authority. There is the right to declare to someone else what is true – in this case what is right and what wrong, and to demand that he accept what one says and act accordingly. There is the authority of superior knowledge – in this case, it would be the authority, i.e. the outstanding credibility, of an expert on right and wrong, virtue and vice. There is again the authority of someone exercising his prophetical office, who teaches *qua* one set up by God to teach; in this case, declaring what is right or wrong, virtuous or vicious.

Now the first of these, however distasteful it may be, is a sort of authority that can hardly be denied to exist by the most recalcitrant modern philosopher. For it is exercised by people in bringing up children; and if there is such a thing as authority of a commanding kind at all, or if there is such a thing as a right, this authority and this right can hardly be denied, since it is quite necessary, if children are to be brought up, that their bringers-up act as if they were exercising such an authority; and since what is a necessity can hardly fail to be a right, so anyone who has to bring children up must have this right.

This authority, however, is not accompanied by any guarantee that someone exercising it will be right in what he teaches. When he is wrong, then, what is the position as regards his authority? To say he still has the right to demand that he be believed is absurd; for there can be no right to be believed when what one says is not right, and no right to demand what one does not have a right to obtain. It would commonly be said that such a person – a parent, say, with erroneous convictions about right and wrong – has a right to be obeyed as far as external actions were concerned, so long as what he demanded was not wrong, or very burdensome and unreasonable. However, I am not interested in that, but only in the character of his authority in declaring what is right or wrong and requiring that his children accept what he says. Authority seems a relatively clear notion when it means the right to be obeyed, even if you are wrong in giving the order, as it does when authority over actions is what we are considering. But it is much more difficult to explain authority to teach, such as a parent exercises in bringing up his children. If this is an authority that he only has when he is right, then, it may be asked, how is it authority at all? The child only has to think him wrong, in order to have to reject his authority: this is to say, for the child to

Paper read at a conference at Bec Abbey in Normandy in 1960 and published in John Todd (ed.) *Problems of Authority* (Darton, Longman and Todd, London, 1962).

think him wrong must lead to the child's rejecting his authority, if the child is logical. But then how can it be a reproach to the child that it did not believe what he said, and so dishonoured its father's authority? And if it cannot, in what sense is there authority here?

Or does authority to teach, such as a parent has – and which he must have inasmuch as he positively has a duty to teach – after all *not* carry with it a right to be believed? But does it not carry a right to demand belief? A right, for example, to order a child to stop being silly?

Nevertheless there is a difference between saying: You did not do as I told you, and that is bad, because it was I, whom you ought to obey, who told you, and: You did not believe what I said, and that is bad, because it was I, whom you ought to believe, who told you.

The difference lies in this: that the one with authority over what you do, can decide, within limits, what you shall do; his decision is what makes it right for you to do what he says – if the reproach against you, when you disobey him, is only that of disobedience. But someone with authority over what you think is not at liberty, within limits, to decide what you shall think among the range of possible thoughts on a given matter; what makes it right for you to think what you think, given that it is your business to form a judgement at all, is simply that it is true, and no decision can make something a true thing for you to think, as the decision of someone in authority can make something a good thing for you to do.

This comes out in the fact that one tells the person under one's authority to do thus and so, but, more often, not: to believe this and that, so much as: that this and that is true. The demand that a child accept what one says is based on the claim to know what he does not and to have the job of telling him. "Why ought I to do that?" – "Because I say so"; if "Why ought I to believe that?" is answered by "Because I say so", that can only be because my saying so is good evidence that the thing is true, and in general it would not be so answered.

Thus, while it is possible to beg or counsel someone to believe something while admitting that one does not believe it oneself, it is not possible authoritatively to order someone to believe something while admitting that one does not believe it oneself. (There are plenty of situations in which one may intelligibly order someone to believe or not to believe something; I will not elaborate them.)

This is connected with the fact that to teach authoritatively is primarily to declare the things one is teaching, demanding attention and mastery of what one says from one's pupil. Now "such-and-such is the case, but I do not believe it is" is notoriously a logical absurdity, even though of a rather curious sort.

So far, our problems have been concerned with the authority of a fallible teacher, whatever he is teaching, not especially with the teaching of morals. But morals I suppose are what is most universally taught by fallible teachers informally at least, by praising and blaming other people, by reining the child in or giving him free rein in various ways (encouragement, reward, etc. and their opposites).

It looks both necessary and impossible that there should be teaching authority on the part of fallible people. A professional teacher, however, presumably has authority to teach; and this does not seem so difficult. Naturally he cannot justifiably claim his teaching commission in support of his teaching when what he teaches is untrue. So he too has a commission only to teach what is true. But the child who will not learn what the teacher teaches – is he not guilty of rejection of authority? And to learn is necessarily to accept, i.e. to believe, a good deal of what one is taught. If a child were liable not to believe his teacher, how could it happen that he selected only those things to disbelieve that were in fact untrue? So he needs to be liable to believe his teacher. If he is, he will learn at any rate some truth; by its aid he will eventually be able to reject what he is taught that is false so far as it is important that he should: or so it is to be hoped.

The right that a fallible teacher has, in that he has authority, then, is the right that those he has to teach should be generally prepared to believe their teachers. At all frequent disbelief when what he says is true will be, then, an injury done to the authority of a teacher – as well as having about it whatever badness attaches to being wrong without excuse.

The great assumption lying behind this is that no one who is taught at all can fail to be taught a great deal that is true and that to a great extent *verum index sui et falsi*.

We sometimes imagine someone with a terribly bad upbringing, who is taught all sorts of misbehaviour as right, and taught to despise much that is good, and we think: what about such a person? But people of the most horrible principles know quite well how to cry out against injustice and lying and treachery, say, when their enemies are guilty of them. So they in fact know quite a lot.

There need not be some common kernel of morals that everyone learns who learns anything. The moral law is a range; some people have one part of the range, some another.

But is there something essentially less teachable about morals than, say, chemistry or history or mathematics – or, again, religious dogma? This view might be maintained in connection with that *autonomy of the will* about which Kant wrote. To take one's morality from someone else – that, it might be held, would make it not morality at all; if one takes it from someone else, that turns it into a bastard sort of morality, marked by heteronomy.

Now it was wrong, in the list of teachable things with which to contrast morality, to put mathematics alongside the others. "Be ye doers of the word and not hearers only" I once saw as the motto of a chapter in a big textbook of higher mathematics, and it was right; one does not learn mathematics by learning that mathematical propositions are truths, but by working out their proofs. Similarly it might be held that one's morality *must* be something one has formulated for oneself, seeing the rightness and wrongness of each of the things one judges to be right or wrong; so that if ever anyone else taught one, he was the occasion of one's formulating for oneself what he taught, rather than the source of information.

There is tied up with this view the idea that one's own personal conscience is necessarily the supreme arbiter in matters of right and wrong. And here we are often not clear whether the necessity is a logical necessity, or a necessity under pain of doing ill: whether, in entertaining the idea of not going by one's own conscience, one is supposed to be guilty of a linguistic absurdity or a reprehensible departure from the right way.

There is a confusion here. Let conscience be one's judgement of right and wrong, i.e. of good and evil in conduct, of what is virtuous and what vicious to do. Then to say that one's own conscience is necessarily supreme arbiter in such matters is to say that necessarily what one judges right and wrong, one judges right and wrong.

One could similarly say that one cannot think anything to be true without thinking it. But that does not tend to show that one cannot think a thing on the strength of what someone else says, judging that that is much more likely than what one could have been inclined to think if left to oneself.

The confusion can perhaps be best cleared up if we consider the parallel case of memory. I can make no judgement about the past without some reliance on my own memory. But only a fool thinks that his own memory is the last word, so far as he is concerned, about what happened. A man may have reason to judge that other men's memory is more reliable than his; and will in any case be well advised to check his own memory against theirs. He may also have reason to believe that some public record is more reliable than his own memory. Of course he would not have any basis for such judgements if he did not already rely on his own memory to some extent; but it would not be reasonable to argue from this that his own memory must after all be for him the last word about what has happened in the past.

Similarly, in practical matters, a man must put some reliance on his own conscience: that is to say, on those judgements of right and wrong which he makes for himself. I call it a judgement that he makes for himself when he judges on a ground that he can see for himself; he does not merely judge "that is wrong", he judges "that is wrong because . . ." and then follows some further account of the action, which he can judge and which he also judges to make the action wrong. To rely exclusively on one's own conscience (one's 'unaided' conscience) is to refuse to judge anything in practical matters unless in this sense one is able to judge for oneself. Now in this sense of "one's own conscience" only a foolish person thinks that his own conscience is the last word, so far as he is concerned, about what to do. For just as any reasonable man knows that his memory may sometimes deceive him, any reasonable man knows that what one has conscientiously decided on one may later conscientiously regret. A man may have reason to judge that another man's moral counsel is more reliable than his own unaided conscience; he will in any case be well advised to take counsel with others; he may, moreover, have reason to believe that some public source of moral teaching is more reliable than his own unaided judgement. Of course he would not have any basis for such judgements if he did not already rely on his own moral judgements to some extent; but it would be sophistical to argue from this that his own conscience must after all be for him the last word about what he ought to do. This sophism, though, aided by confusion with the sense in which it is indeed impossible to take anything but one's conscience as arbiter of right and wrong, has led people to embrace Kant's thesis on the autonomy of the will and to attack, either as illogical or as reprehensible, those who, say, consult the Divine Law and accept its judgements, though themselves unable to see why, say, something forbidden by that law is wrong.

A strong sense of duty may attach to the deliveries of one's conscience – whether they are the deliveries of the 'unaided' conscience or are one's ultimate decision. Some people think that this sense of duty is to be un-questioningly obeyed and that such obedience is a moral vindication. But it is not reasonable to hold that one can so easily get away with having thought good what was bad and bad what was good, and acted accordingly – by having had a sense of duty in connection with what one did. It would have an adverse effect on the seriousness of one's concern to avoid sinning, if one was guaranteed against it by following one's sense of duty – no matter what road it led one on. I do not mean that it would necessarily make one worry less; in some circumstances it might make one worry more; for only an endlessly conscientious style in one's behaviour, only endless bellyaching, could reassure one that one was exercising the sense of duty. Nevertheless that isn't seriousness.

To return to the comparison with mathematics. That suggested that as one cannot just take mathematical information but must think for oneself, so one cannot just take moral information but must think it for oneself; this would be reason to think that one could not be taught morality except in the sense that one can be taught mathematics.

Now there is something right about the comparison. But it is rightly made, not as I made it, by speaking of formulating one's morality for oneself, but as the mathematical textbook made it, by quoting the text from St James: "Be doers of the word and not hearers only."

You have to do the mathematics; and the teacher can get you to do it: that is what teaching mathematics is. Similarly teaching morals will be, not getting the pupil to think something, not giving him a statement to believe, but getting him to act; this can be done by someone who brings up children. One does not learn mathematics, I said, by learning that certain propositions – mathematical ones – are true, but by working out their proofs. Similarly one does not learn morality by learning that certain propositions – ethical ones – are true, but by learning what to do or abstain from in particular situations and getting by practice to do certain things, and abstain from others.

However, the reckoning what to do or abstain from in particular circumstances will constantly include a reference, implicit or explicit, to
generalities. So much so, that this seems to be an important part of what
makes morality. Because of it human conduct is not left to be distinguished
from the behaviour of other animals by the fact that in it calculation is used
by which to ascertain the means to perfectly particular ends. The human
wants things like health and happiness and science and fair repute and virtue
and prosperity, he does not simply want, e.g., that such-and-such a thing
should be in such-and-such a place at such-and-such a time. Such
generalities or principles are: to do good and avoid doing harm; not to do
what will get you disrepute; not to do what will make you poorer; not to take
other people's property. And the questions arise, which of such principles
are true and which false, which quite general and which to be modified in
suitable circumstances; whether indeed they can be called true and false,
right and wrong, and why; what should be the application of this or that one
in describable particular situations. Even if the purpose of such a theory is, as
Aristotle says, not knowledge but practice, the considerations are theoretical
in the sense that they are capable of being argued in the study. A human
being can be brought up without any such study-theory, but the study-
theory of some of the people who have gone in for that kind of thing is liable
in the long run to exert an influence on the practical principles of the general
run of people. If parents teach their children to be reflective, they may
themselves teach them a certain amount of moral theory, and if there is such
a thing as a public teaching, it is likely to be in great part theoretical, i.e.
general, leaving individuals and their advisers to make applications.

Now there is indeed a sense in which only the individual can make his own
decisions as to what to do, even if his decision is to abide by someone else's
orders or advice. For it is he who acts and therefore makes the final application of whatever is said to him.

It may be said, concerning his judgements in the field of theoretical
morals, that in the same way it is he who thinks what he thinks, and so too
only he can make his own decisions as to what to think. No doubt; but here
there is such a thing as believing what he is told without reflection, consideration or interpretation; doing what one is told is an interpretation and
so with doing, however obedient one is, one can hardly escape being one's
own pilot. I have said that a man would be foolish who would not take
advice; but there comes a point where he must act and that is the end of
listening to advice. But with believing it is otherwise; a man may decline to be
his own pilot for certain of his beliefs and altogether rely on authority,
without doing anything on his own account to digest and assimilate the
beliefs. This would be possible in moral matters only to the extent that his
beliefs were idle, without consequences, i.e. if they concerned matters that he
never had to deal with.

Now some dogmatic beliefs are revealed and could not be known otherwise. The question arises whether this could be essential to some moral beliefs. That is to say, whether there are any that are *per se* revealed.

There are two different ways in which a moral belief may be *per accidens* revealed. One way is when someone relies on an authority for something that a man could have thought out for himself. He does not know, let us suppose, whether it is all right at all to beat a child for its misbehaviour. So he asks a modern educationist, supposing him to know, and gets the answer: no; or, if he has different predilections, he consults the Bible and gets the answer: yes. He forms his opinion accordingly. Note that if he is to *act* on it, and the opinion he has adopted is the positive one, he has got to be his own pilot in deciding when and where. But at present we are speaking only of belief, which may perhaps never come to practice. Here, then, is one way in which a moral belief may rely *per accidens* on authority, whether on the authority of an expert (someone supposed to be wise in the field, though of course not supposed to be infallible) or on that of someone with a prophetical office.

Another way is this: some of the facts, of what is the case, will help to determine moral truth – i.e. some of the truth about what is the case will help determine truth about what kinds of thing ought and ought not to be done. Now some such truths about what is the case are revealed; original sin for example. There are also revealed some conditional promises, to disregard which is to despise the goodness of God. Both of these things lead us to infer the rightness of an asceticism which would otherwise have been morbid or founded on a false view of life. Here then is something one could not have worked out for oneself: the furthest one could have got would be to see the advisability of weighting the scales a certain amount against the pleasures and enjoyments of life, as they can be seen to have a practical tendency to corrupt people, i.e. to soften them, make them greedy and pervert and coarsen their judgement. But this would not justify anything severely ascetical.

Here there is room for accepting authority also on the moral conclusions to be drawn from the facts; but *this* acceptance – the acceptance of *consequences* as following – is similar to the acceptance in the first type of *per accidens* revelation of moral truth, just as the grounds on which the authority itself tells you moral truth may be either *per se* revealed truth as to facts, or facts discoverable by reason's unaided investigation.

What there does not seem to be room for is moral truths which are *per se* revealed. Given the facts about original sin and the promise of the possibility of a man's joining his sufferings to those of Christ, the goodness of severely ascetical practices, so long as they do not damage the body or its faculties, is obvious; there is no such thing as a revelation that such-and-such is good or bad not for any reason, not because of any facts, not because of any hopes or prospects, but simply: such-and-such is good to do, this is to be believed, and could not be known or inferred from anything else. How can one instruct an archer to aim at an unseen target? There would be no room for that knowledge by connaturality which is characteristic of the understanding of a virtuous person, in such a case; no room, therefore, for understanding application of what one believed to be right or wrong.

Mr Michael Dummett, reasoning on the topic of cause and effect, came to the conclusion that, but for the goodness of God in revealing it to us, it could not have been known that it would be wrong to engage in certain practices whose object it was to procure that such-and-such should *have* been the case; we might have discovered that something always turned out to have been the case if we subsequently recited some formula, and so recite the formula in order to secure that the past was as we wanted it to have been. Now this is a case in point. If it is not unreasonable, if it is not foolish and superstitious to do this, then there could be nothing wrong with it and there is no room for the exercise of the goodness of God simply in forbidding it. To do it would only be *malum quia prohibitum*.

DISCUSSION

It was objected that the 'new law' of Christ was indeed a revelation in the domain of morality. The speaker admitted this in the sense that the motives, spirit, meaning and purpose of the moral life of Christians depended on revelation, while insisting both that the law of love had already been taught in the Old Testament and that the *content* of the moral law, i.e. the actions which are good and just, is not essentially a matter of revelation.

6   War and Murder

The Use of Violence by Rulers

Since there are always thieves and frauds and men who commit violent attacks on their neighbours and murderers, and since without law backed by adequate force there are usually gangs of bandits; and since there are in most places laws administered by people who command violence to enforce the laws against law-breakers; the question arises: what is a just attitude to this exercise of violent coercive power on the part of rulers and their subordinate officers?

Two attitudes are possible: one, that the world is an absolute jungle and that the exercise of coercive power by rulers is only a manifestation of this; and the other, that it is both necessary and right that there should be this exercise of power, that through it the world is much less of a jungle than it could possibly be without it, so that one should in principle be glad of the existence of such power, and only take exception to its unjust exercise.

It is so clear that the world is less of a jungle because of rulers and laws, and that the exercise of coercive power is essential to these institutions as they are now – all this is so obvious, that probably only Tennysonian conceptions of progress enable people who do not wish to separate themselves from the world to think that nevertheless such violence is objectionable, that some day, in this present dispensation, we shall do without it, and that the pacifist is the man who sees and tries to follow the ideal course, which future civilization must one day pursue. It is an illusion, which would be fantastic if it were not so familiar.

In a peaceful and law abiding country such as England, it may not be immediately obvious that the rulers need to command violence to the point of fighting to the death those that would oppose it; but brief reflection shows that this is so. For those who oppose the force that backs law will not always stop short of fighting to the death and cannot always be put down short of fighting to the death.

Then only if it is in itself evil violently to coerce resistant wills, can the exercise of coercive power by rulers be bad as such. Against such a conception, if it were true, the necessity and advantage of the exercise of such power would indeed be a useless plea. But that conception is one that makes no sense unless it is accompanied by a theory of withdrawal from the world as man's only salvation; and it is in any case a false one. We are taught that God retains the evil will of the devil within limits by violence: we are not given a picture of God permitting to the devil all that he is capable of. There is current a conception of Christianity as having revealed that the defeat of evil

From Walter Stein (ed.), *Nuclear Weapons: A Catholic Response* (London and New York, 1961).

must always be by pure love without coercion; this at least is shown to be false by the foregoing consideration. And without the alleged revelation there could be no reason to believe such a thing.

To think that society's coercive authority is evil is akin to thinking the flesh evil and family life evil. These things belong to the present constitution of mankind; and if the exercise of coercive power is a manifestation of evil, and not the just means of restraining it, then human nature is totally depraved in a manner never taught by Christianity. For society is essential to human good; and society without coercive power is generally impossible.

The same authority which puts down internal dissension, which promulgates laws and restrains those who break them if it can, must equally oppose external enemies. These do not merely comprise those who attack the borders of the people ruled by the authority; but also, for example, pirates and desert bandits, and, generally, those beyond the confines of the country ruled whose activities are viciously harmful to it. The Romans, once their rule in Gaul was established, were eminently justified in attacking Britain, where were nurtured the Druids whose pupils infested northern Gaul and whose practices struck the Romans themselves as *"dira immanitas"*. Further, there being such a thing as the common good of mankind, and visible criminality against it, how can we doubt the excellence of such a proceeding as that violent suppression of the man-stealing business[1] which the British government took it into its head to engage in under Palmerston? The present-day conception of 'aggression', like so many strongly influential conceptions, is a bad one. Why *must* it be wrong to strike the first blow in a struggle? The only question is, who is in the right, if anyone is.

Here, however, human pride, malice and cruelty are so usual that it is true to say that wars have mostly been mere wickedness on both sides. Just as an individual will constantly think himself in the right, whatever he does, and yet there is still such a thing as being in the right, so nations will constantly wrongly think themselves to be in the right – and yet there is still such a thing as their being in the right. Palmerston doubtless had no doubts in prosecuting the opium war against China, which was diabolical; just as he exulted in putting down the slavers. But there is no question but that he was a monster in the one thing, and a just man in the other.

The probability is that warfare is injustice, that a life of military service is a bad life "militia or rather malitia", as St Anselm called it. This probability is greater than the probability (which also exists) that membership of a police force will involve malice, because of the character of warfare: the extraordinary occasions it offers for viciously unjust proceedings on the part of military commanders and warring governments, which at the time attract praise and not blame from their people. It is equally the case that the life of a

---

[1] It is ignorance to suppose that it takes modern liberalism to hate and condemn this. It is cursed and subject to the death penalty in the Mosaic law. Under that code, too, runaway slaves of other nations had asylum in Israel.

ruler is usually a vicious life: but that does not show that ruling is as such a vicious activity.

The principal wickedness which is a temptation to those engaged in warfare is the killing of the innocent, which may often be done with impunity and even to the glory of those who do it. In many places and times it has been taken for granted as a natural part of waging war: the commander, and especially the conqueror, massacres people by the thousand, either because this is part of his glory, or as a terrorizing measure, or as part of his tactics.

Innocence and the Right to Kill Intentionally

It is necessary to dwell on the notion of non-innocence here employed. Innocence is a legal notion; but here, the accused is not pronounced guilty under an existing code of law, under which he has been tried by an impartial judge, and therefore made the target of attack. There is hardly a possibility of this; for the administration of justice is something that takes place under the aegis of a sovereign authority; but in warfare – or the putting down by violence of civil disturbance – the sovereign authority is itself engaged as a party to the dispute and is not subject to a further earthly and temporal authority which can judge the issue and pronounce against the accused. The stabler the society, the rarer it will be for the sovereign authority to have to do anything but apprehend its internal enemy and have him tried: but even in the stablest society there are occasions when the authority has to fight its internal enemy to the point of killing, as happens in the struggle with external belligerent forces in international warfare; and then the characterization of its enemy as non-innocent has not been ratified by legal process.

This, however, does not mean that the notion of innocence fails in this situation. What is required, for the people attacked to be non-innocent in the relevant sense, is that they should themselves be engaged in an objectively unjust proceeding which the attacker has the right to make his concern; or – the commonest case – should be unjustly attacking him. Then he can attack them with a view to stopping them; and also their supply lines and armament factories. But people whose mere existence and activity supporting existence by growing crops, making clothes, etc., constitute an impediment to him – such people are innocent and it is murderous to attack them, or make them a target for an attack which he judges will help him towards victory. For murder is the deliberate killing of the innocent, whether for its own sake or as a means to some further end.

The right to attack with a view to killing normally belongs only to rulers and those whom they command to do it. I have argued that it does belong to rulers precisely because of that threat of violent coercion exercised by those in authority which is essential to the existence of civil societies. It ought not to be pretended that rulers and their subordinates do not choose[2] the killing of their enemies as a means, when it has come to fighting in which they are determined to win and their enemies resist to the point of killing: this holds even in internal disturbances.

When a private man struggles with an enemy he has no right to aim to kill him, unless in the circumstances of the attack on him he can be considered as endowed with the authority of the law and the struggle comes to that point. By a "private" man, I mean a man in a society; I am not speaking of men on their own, without government, in remote places; for such men are neither public servants nor 'private'. The plea of self-defence (or the defence of someone else) made by a private man who has killed someone else must in conscience – even if not in law – be a plea that the death of the other was not intended, but was a side effect of the measures taken to ward off the attack. To shoot to kill, to set lethal man-traps, or, say, to lay poison for someone from whom one's life is in danger, are forbidden. The deliberate choice of inflicting death in a struggle is the right only of ruling authorities and their subordinates. (But I do not deal here with rightful rebellion and struggle against usurped authority.)

In saying that a private man may not choose to kill, we are touching on the principle of "double effect". The denial of this has been the corruption of non-Catholic thought, and its abuse the corruption of Catholic thought. Both have disastrous consequences which we shall see. This principle is not accepted in English law: the law is said not usually to distinguish the foreseen and the intended consequences of an action. Thus, if I push a man over a cliff when he is menacing my life, his death is considered as intended by me, but the intention to be justifiable for the sake of self-defence. Yet the lawyers would hardly find the laying of poison tolerable as an act of self-defence, but only killing by a violent action in a moment of violence. Christian moral theologians have taught that even here one may not seek the death of the assailant, but may in default of other ways of self-defence use such violence as will in fact result in his death. The distinction is evidently a fine one in some cases: what, it may be asked, can the intention be, if it can be said to be absent in this case, except a mere wish or desire?

And yet in other cases the distinction is very clear. If I go to prison rather than perform some action, no reasonable person will call the incidental consequences of my refusal – the loss of my job, for example – intentional just because I knew they must happen. And in the case of the administration of a pain-relieving drug in mortal illness, where the doctor knows the drug may very well kill the patient if the illness does not do so first, the distinction is evident; the lack of it has led an English judge to talk nonsense about the administration of the drug's not having *really* been the cause of death in such a

---

[2] The idea that they may lawfully do what they do, but should not *intend* the death of those they attack, has been put forward and, when suitably expressed, may seem high-minded. But someone who can fool himself into this twist of thought will fool himself into justifying anything, however atrocious, by means of it.

case, even though a post mortem shows it was. For everyone understands that it is a very different thing so to administer a drug, and to administer it with the intention of killing. However, the principle of double effect has more important applications in warfare, and I shall return to it later.

The Influence of Pacifism

Pacifism has existed as a considerable movement in English speaking countries ever since the First World War. I take the doctrine of pacifism to be that it is *eo ipso* wrong to fight in wars, not the doctrine that it is wrong to be compelled to, or that any man, or some men, may refuse; and I think it false for the reasons that I have given. But I now want to consider the very remarkable effects it has had: for I believe its influence to have been enormous, far exceeding its influence on its own adherents.

We should note first that pacifism has as its background conscription and enforced military service for all men. Without conscription, pacifism is a private opinion that will keep those who hold it out of armies, which they are in any case not obliged to join. Now universal conscription, except for the most extraordinary reasons, i.e. as a regular habit among most nations, is such a horrid evil that the refusal of it automatically commands a certain amount of respect and sympathy.

We are not here concerned with the pacifism of some peculiar sect which in any case draws apart from the world to a certain extent, but with a pacifism of people in the world, who do not want to be withdrawn from it. For some of these, pacifism is prevented from being a merely theoretical attitude because they are liable to conscription, and so are prepared to resist it; or are able directly to affect the attitude of some who are so liable.

A powerful ingredient in this pacifism is the prevailing image of Christianity. This image commands a sentimental respect among people who have no belief in Christianity, that is to say, in Christian dogmas; yet do have a certain belief in an idea which they conceive to be part of 'true Christianity'. It is therefore important to understand this image of Christianity and to know how false it is. Such understanding is relevant, not merely to those who wish to believe Christianity, but to all who, without the least wish to believe, are yet profoundly influenced by this image of it.

According to this image, Christianity is an ideal and beautiful religion, impracticable except for a few rare characters. It preaches a God of love whom there is no reason to fear; it marks an escape from the conception presented in the Old Testament, of a vindictive and jealous God who will terribly punish his enemies. The 'Christian God' is a *roi fainèant*, whose only triumph is in the Cross; his appeal is to goodness and unselfishness, and to follow him is to act according to the Sermon on the Mount – to turn the other cheek and to offer no resistance to evil. In this account some of the evangelical counsels are chosen as containing the whole of Christian ethics:

that is, they are made into precepts. (Only some of them; it is not likely that someone who deduces the *duty* of pacifism from the Sermon on the Mount and the rebuke to Peter, will agree to take "Give to him that asks of you" equally as a universally binding precept.)

The turning of counsels into precepts results in high-sounding principles. Principles that are mistakenly high and strict are a trap; they may easily lead in the end directly or indirectly to the justification of monstrous things. Thus if the evangelical counsel about poverty were turned into a precept forbidding property owning, people would pay lip service to it as the ideal, while in practice they went in for swindling. "Absolute honesty!" it would be said: "I can respect that – but of course that means having no property; and while I respect those who follow that course, I have to compromise with the sordid world myself." If then one must 'compromise with evil' by owning property and engaging in trade, then the amount of swindling one does will depend on convenience. This imaginary case is paralleled by what is so commonly said: absolute pacifism is an ideal; unable to follow that, and committed to 'compromise with evil', one must go the whole hog and wage war *à outrance*.

The truth about Christianity is that it is a severe and practicable religion, not a beautifully ideal but impracticable one. Its moral precepts (except for the stricter laws about marriage that Christ enacted, abrogating some of the permissions of the Old Law) are those of the Old Testament; and its God is the God of Israel.

It is ignorance of the New Testament that hides this from people. It is characteristic of pacifism to denigrate the Old Testament and exalt the New: something quite contrary to the teaching of the New Testament itself, which always looks back to and leans upon the Old. How typical it is that the words of Christ "You have heard it said, an eye for an eye and a tooth for a tooth, but I say to you . . ." are taken as a repudiation of the ethic of the Old Testament! People seldom look up the occurrence of this phrase in the juridical code of the Old Testament, where it belongs, and is the admirable principle of law for the punishment of certain crimes, such as procuring the wrongful punishment of another by perjury. People often enough *now* cite the phrase to justify private revenge; no doubt this was as often "heard said" when Christ spoke of it. But no justification for this exists in the personal ethic taught by the Old Testament. On the contrary. What do we find? "Seek no revenge" (Leviticus 19: 18), and "If you find your enemy's ox or ass going astray, take it back to him; if you see the ass of someone who hates you lying under his burden, and would forbear to help him; you must help him" (Exodus 23: 4–5). And "If your enemy is hungry, give him food, if thirsty, give him drink" (Proverbs 25: 21).

This is only one example; given space, it would be easy to show how false is the conception of Christ's teaching as *correcting* the religion of the ancient Israelites, and substituting a higher and more 'spiritual' religion for theirs. Now the false picture I have described plays an important part in the pacifist

ethic and in the ethic of the many people who are not pacifists but are influenced by pacifism.

To extract a pacifist doctrine – i.e. a condemnation of the use of force by
the ruling authorities, and of soldiering as a profession – from the
evangelical counsels and the rebuke to Peter, is to disregard what else is in
the New Testament. It is to forget St John's direction to soldiers: "do not
blackmail people; be content with your pay"; and Christ's commendation
of the centurion, who compared his authority over his men to Christ's. On a
pacifist view, this must be much as if a madam in a brothel had said: "I know
what authority is, I tell this girl to do this, and she does it . . ." and Christ
had commended her faith. A centurion was the first Gentile to be baptized;
there is no suggestion in the New Testament that soldiering was regarded as
incompatible with Christianity. The martyrology contains many names of
soldiers whose occasion for martyrdom was not any objection to soldiering,
but a refusal to perform idolatrous acts.

Now, it is one of the most vehement and repeated teachings of the Judaeo-
Christian tradition that the shedding of innocent blood is forbidden by the
divine law. No man may be punished except for his own crime, and those
"whose feet are swift to shed innocent blood" are always represented as
God's enemies.

For a long time the main outlines of this teaching have seemed to be
merely obvious morality: hence, for example, I have read a passage by
Ronald Knox complaining of the "endless moralizing", interspersed in
records of meanness, cowardice, spite, cruelty, treachery and murder, which
forms so much of the Old Testament. And indeed, that it is terrible to kill the
innocent is very obvious; the morality that so stringently forbids it must
make a great appeal to mankind, especially to the poor threatened victims.
Why should it need the thunder of Sinai and the suffering and preaching of
the prophets to promulgate such a law? But human pride and malice are
everywhere so strong that now, with the fading of Christianity from the mind
of the West, this morality once more stands out as a demand which strikes
pride- and fear-ridden people as too intransigent. For Knox, it seemed so
obvious as to be dull; and he failed to recognize the bloody and beastly
records that it accompanies for the dry truthfulness about human beings that
so characterizes the Old Testament.[3]

Now pacifism teaches people to make no distinction between the shedding
of innocent blood and the shedding of any human blood. And in this way
pacifism has corrupted enormous numbers of people who will not act according to its tenets. They become convinced that a number of things are wicked
which are not; hence seeing no way of avoiding wickedness, they set no
limits to it. How endlessly pacifists argue that all war must be *à outrance*! that
those who wage war must go as far as technological advance permits in the

[3] It is perhaps necessary to remark that I am not here adverting to the total extermination of
certain named tribes of Canaan that is said by the Old Testament to have been commanded by
God. That is something quite outside the provisions of the Mosaic Law for dealings in war.

destruction of the enemy's people. As if the Napoleonic wars were perforce fuller of massacres than the French war of Henry V of England. It is not true: the reverse took place. Nor is technological advance particularly relevant; it is mere squeamishness that deters people who would consent to area bombing from the enormous massacres *by hand* that used once to be committed.

The policy of obliterating cities was adopted by the Allies in the last war; they need not have taken that step, and it was taken largely out of a villainous hatred, and as corollary to the policy, now universally denigrated, of seeking "unconditional surrender". (That policy itself was visibly wicked, and could be and was judged so at the time; it is not surprising that it led to disastrous consequences, even if no one was clever and detached enough to foresee this at the time.)

Pacifism and the respect for pacifism is not the only thing that has led to a universal forgetfulness of the law against killing the innocent; but it has had a share in it.

The Principle of Double Effect

Catholics, however, can hardly avoid paying at least lip-service to that law. So we must ask: how is it that there has been so comparatively little conscience exercised on the subject among them? The answer is: double-think about double effect.

The distinction between the intended, and the merely foreseen, effects of a voluntary action is indeed absolutely essential to Christian ethics. For Christianity forbids a number of things as being bad in themselves. But if I am answerable for the foreseen consequences of an action or refusal, as much as for the action itself, then these prohibitions will break down. If someone innocent will die unless I do a wicked thing, then on this view I am his murderer in refusing: so all that is left to me is to weigh up evils. Here the theologian steps in with the principle of double effect and says: "No, you are no murderer, if the man's death was neither your aim nor your chosen means, and if you had to act in the way that led to it or else do something absolutely forbidden." Without understanding of this principle, anything can be – and is wont to be – justified, and the Christian teaching that in no circumstances may one commit murder, adultery, apostasy (to give a few examples) goes by the board. These absolute prohibitions of Christianity by no means exhaust its ethic; there is a large area where what is just is determined partly by a prudent weighing up of consequences. But the prohibitions are bedrock, and without them the Christian ethic goes to pieces. Hence the necessity of the notion of double effect.

At the same time, the principle has been repeatedly abused from the seventeenth century up till now. The causes lie in the history of philosophy. From the seventeenth century till now what may be called Cartesian psychology has dominated the thought of philosophers and theologians. According to this psychology, an intention was an interior act of the mind which could be produced at will. Now if intention is all important – as it is – in determining the goodness or badness of an action, then, on this theory of what intention is, a marvellous way offered itself of making any action lawful. You only had to 'direct your intention' in a suitable way. In practice, this means making a little speech to yourself: "What I mean to be doing is. . .".

This perverse doctrine has occasioned repeated condemnations by the Holy See from the seventeenth century to the present day. Some examples will suffice to show how the thing goes. Typical doctrines from the seventeenth century were that it is all right for a servant to hold the ladder for his criminous master so long as he is merely avoiding the sack by doing so; or that a man might wish for and rejoice at his parent's death so long as what he had in mind was the gain to himself; or that it is not simony to offer money, not *as a price* for the spiritual benefit, but only *as an inducement* to give it. A condemned doctrine from the present day is that the practice of *coitus reservatus* is permissible: such a doctrine could only arise in connection with that 'direction of intention' which sets everything right no matter what one does. A man makes a practice of withdrawing, telling himself that he *intends* not to ejaculate; of course (if that is his practice) he usually does so, but then the event is accidental and *praeter intentionem*: it is, in short, a case of 'double effect'.

This same doctrine is used to prevent any doubts about the obliteration bombing of a city. The devout Catholic bomber secures by a 'direction of intention' that any shedding of innocent blood that occurs is 'accidental'. I know a Catholic boy who was puzzled at being told by his schoolmaster that it was an *accident* that the people of Hiroshima and Nagasaki were there to be killed; in fact, however absurd it seems, such thoughts are common among priests who know that they are forbidden by the divine law to justify the direct killing of the innocent.

It is nonsense to pretend that you do not intend to do what is the means you take to your chosen end. Otherwise there is absolutely no substance to the Pauline teaching that we may not do evil that good may come.

Some Commonly Heard Arguments

There are a number of sophistical arguments often or sometimes used on these topics, which need answering.

Where do you draw the line? As Dr Johnson said, the fact of twilight does not mean you cannot tell day from night. There are borderline cases, where it is difficult to distinguish, in what is done, between means and what is incidental to, yet in the circumstances inseparable from, those means. The obliteration bombing of a city is not a borderline case.

The old "conditions for a just war" are irrelevant to the conditions of modern warfare, so that must be condemned out of hand: People who say this always envisage only major wars between the Great Powers, which Powers are indeed now "in blood stepp'd in so far" that it is unimaginable for there to be a war between them which is not a set of enormous massacres of civil populations. But these are not the only wars. Why is Finland so far free? At least partly because of the "posture of military preparedness" which, considering the character of the country, would have made subjugating the Finns a difficult and unrewarding task. The offensive of the Israelis against the Egyptians in 1956 involved no plan of making civil populations the target of military attack.

In a modern war the distinction between combatants and non-combatants is meaningless, so an attack on anyone on the enemy side is justified: This is pure nonsense; even in war, a very large number of the enemy population are just engaged in maintaining the life of the country, or are sick, or aged or children.

It must be legitimate to maintain an opinion – viz. that the destruction of cities by bombing is lawful – if this is argued by competent theologians and the Holy See has not pronounced: The argument from the silence of the Holy See has itself been condemned by the Holy See (Denzinger, 28th Edition, 1127). How could this be a sane doctrine in view of the endless twistiness of the human mind?

Whether a war is just or not is not for the private man to judge: he must obey his government: Sometimes, this may be; especially as far as concerns causes of war. But the individual who joins in destroying a city, like a Nazi massacring the inhabitants of a village, is too obviously marked out as an enemy of the human race, to shelter behind such a plea.

Finally, horrible as it is to have to notice this, we must notice that even the arguments about double effect – which at least show that a man is not willing openly to justify the killing of the innocent – are now beginning to look old-fashioned. Some Catholics are not scrupling to say that *anything* is justified in defence of the continued existence and liberty of the Church in the West. A terrible fear of communism drives people to say this sort of thing. "Our Lord told us to fear those who can destroy body and soul, not to fear the destruction of the body" was blasphemously said to a friend of mine; meaning: "so, we must fear Russian domination more than the destruction of people's bodies by obliteration bombing."

But whom did Our Lord tell us to fear, when he said: "I will tell you whom you shall fear" and "Fear not them that can destroy the body, but fear him who can destroy body and soul in hell"? He told us to fear God the Father, who can and will destroy the unrepentant disobedient, body and soul, in hell.

A Catholic who is tempted to think on the lines I have described should remember that the Church is the spiritual Israel: that is to say, that Catholics are what the ancient Jews were, salt for the earth and the people of

God – and that what was true of some devout Jews of ancient times can equally well be true of us now: "You compass land and sea to make a convert, and when you have done so, you make him twice as much a child of hell as yourselves." Do Catholics sometimes think that they are immune to such a possibility? That the Pharisees – who sat in the seat of Moses and who were so zealous for the true religion – were bad in ways in which we cannot be bad if we are zealous? I believe they do. But our faith teaches no such immunity, it teaches the opposite. "We are in danger all our lives long." So we have to fear God and keep his commandments, and calculate what is for the best only within the limits of that obedience, knowing that the future is in God's power and that no one can snatch away those whom the Father has given to Christ.

It is not a vague faith in the triumph of the spirit over force (there is little enough warrant for that), but a definite faith in the divine promises, that makes us believe that the Church canot fail. Those, therefore, who think they must be prepared to wage a war with Russia involving the deliberate massacre of cities, must be prepared to say to God: "We had to break your law, lest your Church fail. We could not obey your commandments, for we did not believe your promises."

7 Mr Truman's Degree

I

In 1939, on the outbreak of war, the President of the United States asked for assurances from the belligerent nations that civil populations would not be attacked.

In 1945, when the Japanese enemy was known by him to have made two attempts towards a negotiated peace, the President of the United States gave the order for dropping an atom bomb on a Japanese city; three days later a second bomb, of a different type, was dropped on another city. No ultimatum was delivered before the second bomb was dropped.

Set side by side, these events provide enough of a contrast to provoke enquiry. Evidently development has taken place; one would like to see its course plotted. It is not, I think, difficult to give an intelligible account:

(1) The British Government gave President Roosevelt the required assurance with a reservation which meant "If the Germans do it we shall do it too." You don't promise to abide by the Queensberry Rules even if your opponent abandons them.

(2) The only condition for ending the war was announced to be unconditional surrender. Apart from the "liberation of the subject peoples", the objectives were vague in character. Now the demand for unconditional surrender was mixed up with a determination to make no peace with Hitler's government. In view of the character of Hitler's regime that attitude was very intelligible. Nevertheless some people have doubts about it now. It is suggested that defeat of itself would have resulted in the rapid discredit and downfall of that government. On this I can form no strong opinion. The important question to my mind is whether the intention of making no peace with Hitler's government necessarily entailed the objective of unconditional surrender. If, as may not be impossible, we could have formulated a pretty definite objective, a rough outline of the terms which we were willing to make with Germany, while at the same time indicating that we would not make terms with Hitler's government, then the question of the wisdom of this latter demand seems to me a minor one; but if not, then that settles it. It was the insistence on unconditional surrender that was the root of all evil. The connection between such a demand and the need to use the most ferocious methods of warfare will be obvious. And in itself the proposal of an unlimited objective in war is stupid and barbarous.

(3) The Germans did a good deal of indiscriminate bombing in this country. It is impossible for an uninformed person to know how much, in its first beginnings, was due to indifference on the part of pilots to using their

Pamphlet published by the author (Oxford, 1957).

loads only on military targets, and how much to actual policy on the part of those who sent them. Nor do I know what we were doing in the same line at the time. But certainly anyone would have been stupid who had thought in 1939 that there would not be such bombing, developing into definite raids on cities.

(4) For some time before war broke out, and more intensely afterwards, there was propaganda in this country on the subject of the "indivisibility" of modern war. The civilian population, we were told, is really as much combatant as the fighting forces. The military strength of a nation includes its whole economic and social strength. Therefore the distinction between the people engaged in prosecuting the war and the population at large is unreal. There is no such thing as a non-participator; you cannot buy a postage stamp or any taxed article, or grow a potato or cook a meal, without contributing to the "war effort". War indeed is a "ghastly evil", but once it has broken out no one can "contract out" of it. "Wrong" indeed must be being done if war is waged, but you cannot help being involved in it. There was a doctrine of "collective responsibility" with a lugubriously elevated moral tone about it. The upshot was that it was senseless to draw any line between legitimate and illegitimate objects of attack. Thus the court chaplains of the democracy. I am not sure how children and the aged fitted into this story: probably they cheered the soldiers and munitions workers up.

(5) The Japanese attacked Pearl Harbour and there was war between America and Japan. Some American (Republican) historians now claim that the acknowledged fact that the American Government knew an attack was impending some hours before it occurred, but did not alert the people in local command, can only be explained by a purpose of arousing the passions of American people. However that may be, those passions were suitably aroused and the war was entered on with the same vague and hence limitless objectives; and once more unconditional surrender was the only condition on which the war was going to end.

(6) Then came the great change: we adopted the system of 'area bombing' as opposed to 'target bombing'. This differed from even big raids on cities, such as had previously taken place in the course of the war, by being far more extensive and devastating and much less random; the whole of a city area would be systematically plotted out and dotted with bombs. "Attila was a Sissy", as the *Chicago Tribune* headed an article on this subject.

(7) In 1945, at the Potsdam conference in July, Stalin informed the American and British statesmen that he had received two requests from the Japanese to act as a mediator with a view to ending the war. He had refused. The Allies agreed on the "general principle" – marvellous phrase! – of using the new type of weapon that America now possessed. The Japanese were given a chance in the form of the Potsdam Declaration, calling for unconditional surrender in face of overwhelming force soon to be arrayed against them. The historian of the Survey of International Affairs considers that this phrase was rendered meaningless by the statement of a series of terms; but of

these the ones incorporating the Allies' demands were mostly of so vague and sweeping a nature as to be rather a declaration of what unconditional surrender would be like than to constitute conditions. It seems to be generally agreed that the Japanese were desperate enough to have accepted the Declaration but for their loyalty to their Emperor: the "terms" would certainly have permitted the Allies to get rid of him if they chose. The Japanese refused the Declaration. In consequence, the bombs were dropped on Hiroshima and Nagasaki. The decision to use them on people was Mr Truman's.

For men to choose to kill the innocent as a means to their ends is always murder, and murder is one of the worst of human actions. So the prohibition on deliberately killing prisoners of war or the civilian population is not like the Queensberry Rules: its force does not depend on its promulgation as part of positive law, written down, agreed upon, and adhered to by the parties concerned.

When I say that to choose to kill the innocent as a means to one's ends is murder, I am saying what would generally be accepted as correct. But I shall be asked for my definition of "the innocent". I will give it, but later. Here, it is not necessary; for with Hiroshima and Nagasaki we are not confronted with a borderline case. In the bombing of these cities it was certainly decided to kill the innocent as a means to an end. And a very large number of them, all at once, without warning, without the interstices of escape or the chance to take shelter, which existed even in the 'area bombings' of the German cities.

I have long been puzzled by the common cant about President Truman's courage in making this decision. Of course, I know that you can be cowardly without having reason to think you are in danger. But how can you be courageous? Light has come to me lately: the term is an acknowledgement of the truth. Mr Truman was brave because, and only because, what he did was so bad. But I think the judgement unsound. Given the right circumstances (for example that no one whose opinion matters will disapprove), a quite mediocre person can do spectacularly wicked things without thereby becoming impressive.

I determined to oppose the proposal to give Mr Truman an honorary degree here at Oxford. Now, an honorary degree is not a reward of merit: it is, as it were, a reward for being a very distinguished person, and it would be foolish to enquire whether a candidate deserves to be as distinguished as he is. That is why, in general, the question whether so-and-so should have an honorary degree is devoid of interest. A very distinguished person will hardly be also a notorious criminal, and if he should chance to be a non-notorious criminal it would, in my opinion, be improper to bring the matter up. It is only in the rather rare case in which a man is known everywhere for an action, in face of which it is sycophancy to honour him, that the question can be of the slightest interest.

I have been accused of being "high-minded". I must be saying "You may not do evil that good may come", which is a disagreeably high-minded doctrine. The action was necessary, or at any rate it was thought by competent, expert military opinion to be necessary; it probably saved more lives than it sacrificed; it had a good result, it ended the war. Come now: if you had to choose between boiling one baby and letting some frightful disaster befall a thousand people – or a million people, if a thousand is not enough – what would you do? Are you going to strike an attitude and say "You may not do evil that good may come"? (People who never hear such arguments will hardly believe they take place, and will pass this rapidly by.)

"It pretty certainly saved a huge number of lives". Given the conditions, I agree. That is to say, if those bombs had not been dropped the Allies would have had to invade Japan to achieve their aim, and they would have done so. Very many soldiers on both sides would have been killed; the Japanese, it is said – and it may well be true – would have massacred the prisoners of war; and large numbers of their civilian population would have been killed by 'ordinary' bombing.

I do not dispute it. Given the conditions, that was probably what was averted by that action. But what were the conditions? The unlimited objective, the fixation on unconditional surrender. The disregard of the fact that the Japanese were desirous of negotiating peace. The character of the Potsdam Declaration – their 'chance'. I will not suggest, as some would like to do, that there was an exultant itch to use the new weapons, but it seems plausible to think that the consciousness of the possession of such instruments had its effect on the manner in which the Japanese were offered their 'chance'.

We can now reformulate the principle of doing evil that good may come: every fool can be as much of a knave as suits him.

I recommend this history to undergraduates reading Greats as throwing a glaring light on Aristotle's thesis that you cannot be or do any good where you are stupid.

I informed the Senior Proctor of my intention to oppose Mr Truman's degree. He consulted the Registrar to get me informed on procedure. The Vice-Chancellor was informed; I was cautiously asked if I had got up a party. I had not; but a fine House was whipped up to vote for the honour. The dons at St John's were simply told "The women are up to something in Convocation; we have to go and vote them down". In Worcester, in All Souls, in New College, however, consciences were greatly exercised, as I have heard. A reason was found to satisfy them: *It would be wrong to try to PUNISH Mr Truman!* I must say I rather like St John's.

The Censor of St Catherine's had an odious task. He must make a speech which should pretend to show that a couple of massacres to a man's credit are not exactly a reason for not showing him honour. He had, however, one great advantage: he did not have to persuade his audience, who were already perfectly convinced of that proposition. But at any rate he had to make a show.

The defence, I think, would not have been well received at Nuremberg.

We do not approve the action; no, we think it was a *mistake*. (That is how communists now talk about Stalin's more murderous proceedings.) Further, Mr Truman did not make the bombs by himself, and decide to drop them without consulting anybody; no, he was only responsible for the decision. Hang it all, you can't make a man responsible just because "his is the signature at the foot of the order". Or was he not even responsible for the decision? It was not quite clear whether Mr Bullock was saying that or not; but I never heard anyone else seem to give the lie to Mr Truman's boasts. Finally, an action of this sort is, after all, only one episode: an incidental, as it were, in a career. Mr Truman has done some good.

I know that in one way such a speech does not deserve scrutiny; after all, it was just something to say on its occasion. And he had to say something. One must not suppose that one can glean anything a man actually thinks from what he says in such circumstances. Professor Stebbing exposing the logical fallacies in politicians' speeches is a comic spectacle.

II

Choosing to kill the innocent as a means to your ends is always murder. Naturally, killing the innocent as an end in itself is murder too; but that is no more than a possible future development for us:[1] in our part of the globe it is a practice that has so far been confined to the Nazis. I intend my formulation to be taken strictly; each term in it is necessary. For killing the innocent, even if you know as a matter of statistical certainty that the things you do involve it, is not necessarily murder. I mean that if you attack a lot of military targets, such as munitions factories and naval dockyards, as carefully as you can, you will be certain to kill a number of innocent people; but that is not murder. On the other hand, unscrupulousness in considering the possibilities turns it into murder. I here print as a case in point a letter which I received lately from Holland:

> We read in our paper about your opposition to Truman. I do not like him either, but do you know that in the war the English bombed the dykes of our province Zeeland, an island where nobody could escape anywhere to. Where the whole population was drowned, children, women, farmers working in the field, all the cattle, everything, hundreds and hundreds, and we were your allies! Nobody ever speaks about that. Perhaps it were well to know this. Or, to remember.

That was to trap some fleeing German military. I think my correspondent has something.

It may be impossible to take the thing (or people) you want to destroy as your target; it may be possible to attack it only by taking as the object of your attack what includes large numbers of innocent people. Then you cannot very well say they died by accident. Here your action is murder.

[1] This will seem a preposterous assertion; but we are certainly on the way, and I can think of no reasons for confidence that it will not happen.

"But where will you draw the line? It is impossible to draw an exact line." This is a common and absurd argument against drawing any line; it may be very difficult, and there are obviously borderline cases. But we have fallen into the way of drawing no line, and offering as justifications what an uncaptive mind will find only a bad joke. Wherever the line is, certain things are certainly well to one side or the other of it.

Now who are "the innocent" in war? They are all those who are not fighting and not engaged in supplying those who are with the means of fighting. A farmer growing wheat which may be eaten by the troops is not "supplying them with the means of fighting". Over this, too, the line may be difficult to draw. But that does not mean that no line should be drawn, or that, even if one is in doubt just where to draw the line, one cannot be crystal clear that this or that is well over the line.

"But the people fighting are probably conscripts! In that case they are just as innocent as anyone else." "Innocent" here is not a term referring to personal responsibility at all. It means rather "not harming". But the people fighting are "harming", so they can be attacked; but if they surrender they become in this sense innocent and so may not be maltreated or killed. Nor is there ground for trying them on a criminal charge; not, indeed, because a man has no personal responsibility for fighting, but because they were not the subjects of the state whose prisoners they are.

There is an argument which I know from experience it is necessary to forestall at this point, though I think it is visibly captious. It is this: on my theory, would it not follow that a soldier can only be killed when he is actually attacking? Then, for example, it would be impossible to attack a sleeping camp. The answer is that "what someone is doing" can refer either to what he is doing at the moment or to his role in a situation. A soldier under arms is 'harming' in the latter sense even if he is asleep. But it is true that the enemy should not be attacked more ferociously than is necessary to put them *hors de combat*.

These conceptions are distinct and intelligible ones; they would formerly have been said to belong to the Law of Nations. Anyone can see that they are good, and we pay tribute to them by our moral indignation when our enemies violate them. But in fact they are going, and only fragments of them are left. General Eisenhower, for example, is reported to have spoken slightingly once of the notion of chivalry towards prisoners – as if that were based on respect for their virtue or for the nation from which they come, and not on the fact that they are now defenceless.

It is characteristic of nowadays to talk with horror of killing rather than of murder, and hence, since in war you have committed yourself to killing – for example "accepted an evil" – not to mind whom you kill. This seems largely to be the work of the devil; but I also suspect that it is in part an effect of the existence of pacifism, as a doctrine which many people respect though they would not adopt it. This effect would not exist if people had a distinct notion of what makes pacifism a false doctrine.

It therefore seems to me important to show that for one human being deliberately to kill another is not inevitably wrong. I may seem to be wasting my time, as most people do reject pacifism. But it is nevertheless important to argue the point because if one does so one sees that there are pretty severe restrictions on legitimate killing. Of course, people accept this within the state, but when it comes to war they have the idea that any restrictions are something like the Queensberry Rules – instead of making the difference between being guilty and not guilty of murder.

I will not discuss the self-defence of a private person. If he kills the man who attacks him or someone else, it ought to be accidental. To aim at killing, even when one is defending oneself, is murderous. (I fear even this idea is going. A man was acquitted recently who had successfully set a lethal booby trap to kill a thief in his absence.)

But the state actually has the authority to order deliberate killing in order to protect its people or to put frightful injustices right. (For example, the plight of the Jews under Hitler would have been a reasonable cause of war.) The reason for this is pretty simple: it stands out most clearly if we first consider the state's right to order such killing within its confines. I am not referring to the death penalty, but to what happens when there is rioting or when violent malefactors have to be caught. Rioters can sometimes only be restrained, or malefactors seized, by force. Law without force is ineffectual, and human beings without laws miserable (though we, who have too many and too changeable laws, may easily not feel this very distinctly). So much is indeed fairly obvious, though the more peaceful the society the less obvious it is that the force in the hands of the servants of the law has to be force up to the point of killing. It would become perfectly obvious any time there was rioting or gangsterism which had to be dealt with by the servants of the law fighting.

The death penalty itself is a completely different matter. The state is not fighting the criminal who is condemned to death. That is why the death penalty is not indispensable. People keep on discussing whether the point of it is deterrence or vengeance; it is neither. Not deterrence, because nobody has proved anything about that, and people think what they think in accordance with their prejudices. And not vengeance, because that is nobody's business. Confusion arises on this subject because the state is said, and correctly said, to *punish* the criminal, and "punishment" suggests "vengeance". Therefore many humane people dislike the idea and prefer such notions as "correction" and "rehabilitation". But the action of the state in depriving a man of his rights, up to his very life, has to be considered from two sides. First, from that of the man himself. If he could justly say "Why have you done this to me? I have not deserved it", then the state would be acting with injustice. Therefore he must be proved guilty, and only as punishment has the state the right to inflict anything on him. The concept of punishment is our one safeguard against being done 'good' to, in ways involving a deprivation of rights, by impudent powerful people. Second, from the side of the state, divine retributive justice is not its affair: it only has to protect its people and restrain malefactors. The ground of its right to deprive of liberty and even life is only that the malefactor is a nuisance, like a gangrenous limb. Therefore it can cut him off entirely, if his crime is so bad that he could not justly protest "I have not deserved *this*." But when I say that the sole ground of the state's right to kill him is that he is a nuisance, I only mean that he is a nuisance *qua* malefactor. The lives of the innocent are the actual point of society, so the fact that in some other way they may be a nuisance (troublesome to look after, for example) does not justify the state in getting rid of them. Though that is another thing we may yet come to. But the blood of the innocent cries to heaven for vengeance.

Thus the malefactor who has been found guilty is the only defenceless person whom the state may put to death. It need not; it can choose more merciful laws. (I have no prejudice in favour of the death penalty.) Any other defenceless person is as such innocent, in the sense "not harming". And so the state can only order to kill others of its subjects besides convicted criminals if they are rioting or doing something that has to be stopped, and can only be stopped by the servants of the law fighting them.

Now, this is also the ground of the state's right to order people to fight external enemies who are unjustly attacking them or something of theirs. The right to order to fight for the sake of other people's wrongs, to put right something affecting people who are not actually under the protection of the state, is a rather more dubious thing obviously, but it exists because of the common sympathy of human beings whereby one feels for one's neighbour if he is attacked. So in an attenuated sense it can be said that something that belongs to, or concerns, one is attacked if anybody is unjustly attacked or maltreated.

Pacifism, then, is a false doctrine. Now, no doubt, it is bad just for that reason, because it is always bad to have a false conscience. In this way the doctrine that it is a bad act to lay a bet is bad: it is all right to bet what it is all right to risk or drop in the sea. But I want to maintain that pacifism is a harmful doctrine in a far stronger sense than this. Even the prevalence of the idea that it was wrong to bet would have no particularly bad consequences; a false doctrine which merely forbids what is not actually bad need not encourage people in anything bad. But with pacifism it is quite otherwise. It is a factor in that loss of the conception of murder which is my chief interest in this pamphlet.

I have very often heard people say something like this: "It is all very well to say 'Don't do evil that good may come.' But *war* is evil. We all know that. Now, of course, it is possible to be an Absolute Pacifist. I can respect that, but I can't be one myself, and most other people won't be either. So we have to accept the evil. It is not that we do not see the evil. And once you are in for it, you have to go the whole hog."

This is much as if I were defrauding someone, and when someone tried to stop me I said: "Absolute honesty! I respect that. But of course absolute

honesty really means having no property at all . . ." Having offered the
sacrifice of a few sighs and tears to absolute honesty, I go on as before.

The correct answer to the statement that "war is evil" is that it is bad – for
example a misfortune – to be at war. And no doubt if two nations are at war
at least one is unjust. But that does not show that it is wrong to fight or that if
one does fight one can also commit murder.

Naturally my claim that pacifism is a very harmful doctrine is contingent
on its being a false one. If it were a true doctrine, its encouragement of this
nonsensical 'hypocrisy of the ideal standard' would not count against it.
But given that it is false, I am inclined to think it is also very bad, unusually so
for an idea which seems as it were to err on the noble side.

When I consider the history of events from 1939 to 1945, I am not surprised that Mr Truman is made the recipient of honours. But when I
consider his actions by themselves, I am surprised again.

Some people actually praise the bombings and commend the stockpiling
of atomic weapons on the ground that they are so horrible that nations will
be afraid ever again to make war. "We have made a covenant with death, and
with hell we are at an agreement." There does not seem to be good ground
for such a hope for any long period of time.

Pacifists have for long made it a point in their propaganda that men must
grow more murderous as their techniques of destruction improve, and those
who defend murder eagerly seize on this point, so that I imagine by now it is
pretty well accepted by the whole world. Of course, it is not true. In
Napoleon's time, for example, the means of destruction had much
improved since the time of Henry V; but Henry, not Napoleon, was a great
massacrer of civilians, saying when he did particularly atrocious things that
the French were a sinful nation and that he had a mission from God to
punish them. And, of course, really large scale massacre up to now has
belonged to times with completely primitive methods of killing. Weapons
are now manufactured whose sole point is to be used in massacre of cities.
But the people responsible are not murderous because they have these
weapons; they have them because they are murderous. Deprived of atomic
bombs, they would commit massacres by means of other bombs.

Protests by people who have not power are a waste of time. I was not
seizing an opportunity to make a "gesture of protest" at atomic bombs; I
vehemently object to *our* action in offering Mr Truman honours, because
one can share in the guilt of a bad action by praise and flattery, as also by
defending it. When I puzzle myself over the attitude of the Vice-Chancellor
and the Hebdomadal Council, I look round to see if any explanation is
available why so many Oxford people should be willing to flatter such a
man.

I get some small light on the subject when I consider the productions of
Oxford moral philosophy since the First World War, which I have lately had
occasion to read. Its character can easily be briefly demonstrated. Up to the
Second World War the prevailing moral philosophy in Oxford taught that

an action can be "morally good" no matter how objectionable the thing done may be. An instance would be Himmler's efforts at exterminating the Jews: he did it from the "motive of duty" which has "supreme value". In the same philosophy – which has much pretence of moral seriousness, claiming that "rightness" is an objective character in acts, that can be discerned by a moral sense – it is also held that it might be right to kill the innocent for the good of the people, since the "prima facie duty" of securing some advantage might outweigh the "prima facie duty" of not killing the innocent. This sort of philosophy is less prevalent now, and in its place I find another, whose cardinal principle is that "good" is not a "descriptive" term, but one expressive of a favourable attitude on the part of the speaker. Hand in hand with this, though I do not know if there is any logical connection, goes a doctrine that it is impossible to have any quite general moral laws; such laws as "It is wrong to lie" or "Never commit sodomy" are rules of thumb which an experienced person knows when to break. Further, both his selection of these as the rules on which to proceed, and his tactful adjustments of them in particular cases, are based on their fitting together with the "way of life" which is his preference. Both these philosophies, then, contain a repudiation of the idea that any class of actions, such as murder, may be absolutely excluded. I do not know how influential they may have been or be; they are perhaps rather symptomatic. Whether influential or symptomatic, they throw some light on the situation.

It is possible still to withdraw from this shameful business in some slight degree; it is possible not to go to Encaenia; if it should be embarrassing to someone who would normally go to plead other business, he could take to his bed. I, indeed, should fear to go, in case God's patience suddenly ends.

8 The Justice of the Present War Examined

1 *Introductory*

In these days the authorities claim the right to control not only the policy of the nation but also the actions of every individual within it; and their claim has the support of a large section of the people of the country, and of a peculiar force of emotion. This support is gained, and this emotion caused by the fact that they are "evil things" that we are fighting against. That they are evil we need have no doubt; yet many of us still feel distrust of these claims and these emotions lest they blind men to their duty of considering carefully, before they act, the justice of the things they propose to do. Men can be moved to fight by being made to hate the deeds of their enemies; but a war is not made just by the fact that one's enemies' deeds are hateful. Therefore it is our duty to resist passion and to consider carefully whether all the conditions of a just war are satisfied in this present war, lest we sin against the natural law by participating in it.

2 *The Natural Moral Law*

This idea of natural moral law is one which modern men have lost; but without it they cannot live in peace within themselves, or socially or internationally. For the natural law is the law of man's own nature, showing how he must choose to act in matters where his will is free, if his nature is to be properly fulfilled. It is the proper use of his functions; their misuse or perversion is sin. So, lying is the misuse of speech, and is therefore wicked. So, justice is the proper working out of relations between man and man, and between societies, each having his due.

To those who believe in God it will rightly appear that His law, the eternal law, has its reflection in the ordered activity of Creation, that 'law of nature' which is the truth of things. In man, this activity is not wholly determined, but there is an element of choice. Thus far, "to him the law is proposed; it is not imposed upon him".[1] But it is not less law for that; it binds because it is

[1] Sertillanges, quoted "Moral Principles and Practice", Cambridge Summer School (1932), p. 74.

The first Part (entitled 'The War and the Moral Law') of a pamphlet by G. E. M. Anscombe and Norman Daniel, published by the authors (Oxford, 1939).

the law of his nature. And in what it consists he can discover by reason, checked and guaranteed by the divine revelation of Scripture. Aquinas called it "the participation in the eternal law of the rational creature" (Thomas Aquinas, *Summa Theologica*, 1a 2ae. 91, art. 2 ad 3); the law in him from his creation, which he, making use of the gifts of reason and revelation, will find for his salvation. Thus will he proceed to his eternal destiny in God; but the condition of the love of God is the observance of the natural law; if man does not live according to his proper nature he will not attain his proper end.[2]

With this in mind, let us proceed to consider what is justice in the matter of war, remembering that whatever human hopes for the happiness of mankind may be, the only way to that happiness is an observance of the law of God without any deviation.

3   The Conditions of the Just War

There are seven conditions which must be all fulfilled for a war to be just:

(1) There must be a just occasion: that is, there must be violation of, or attack upon, strict rights.

(2) The war must be made by a lawful authority: that is, when there is no higher authority, a sovereign state.

(3) The warring state must have an upright intention in making war: it must not declare war in order to obtain, or inflict anything unjust.

(4) Only right means must be used in the conduct of the war.

(5) War must be the only possible means of righting the wrong done.

(6) There must be a reasonable hope of victory.

(7) The probable good must outweigh the probable evil effects of the war.[3]

For this present war there is a just occasion; the rights of Poland have been infringed. The war was declared by a lawful authority. There is, so far as we can tell, a reasonable hope of victory. And though we may suspect that war could have been averted by a more intelligent policy up to a very short time before war broke out, yet at the time when war was declared it is possible that the wrong done could not have been righted by peaceful means. But there remain three conditions to be fulfilled: the intentions of our government must be upright, both (1) as to means, and (2) as to ends, and (3) the probable good effects of the war must outweigh the probable evil. If these conditions are not fulfilled, *this* war is rendered wrong, however just the occasion, however desirable that we should fight *a* war. Nor, if we know that a war is wrong, may we take part in it without sin, however grievous it may seem to stand apart from our fellowcountrymen.

We must note that, if we fight a war, it is the government's war, since, as we

[2] For a fuller discussion of the natural law, see Thomas Aquinas, 1a 2ae, 91, 1a 2ae, 94, or any textbook of moral theology.

[3] For sources concerning the conditions of the just war, see J. Eppstein, *Catholic Tradition and the Law of Nations* (London, 1935), and, more fully, Regaut, *La Doctrine de la Guerre Juste*.

have seen, wars can only be made by sovereign states. Therefore we cannot say: "The government's intentions are *vicious*; but the things *I* am fighting for are just," or "The government intends to use evil means, but *I* shall do nothing unjust." A private person may not make war; and if he joins in a war, he joins in it as justified or vitiated by the just or unjust intentions of the government under which he fights. By "government" we mean the persons holding power in a sovereign state. Another point to note is that a government may succumb to temptation in the course of the war; if this involved departure from any of the seven conditions the justice of the war would be vitiated. But isolated pieces of wickedness, though participation in them would be wrong, would not themselves vitiate the whole war on grounds of intention; the probability of such would simply contribute to the balance of evil effects which must be considered.

4   On Aims

If a war is to be just, the warring state must intend only what is just, and the aim of the war must be to set right certain specific injustices. That is, the righting of wrong done must be a sufficient condition on which peace will be made.

In the present war, we may have grave doubts about our government's sincerity. It may seem that we never cared about Poland, but made the Polish treaty as a pretext for seizing the next opportunity to oppose the German government. Our government was badly frightened; it had been weak; it wanted to take a strong line lest it be utterly discredited; and hence the Polish pact. These beginnings are dubious enough; partly because the injustice done to Poland seems our pretext, not our cause, for entering the war; partly because our government appears to have acted from fear and pride, rather than from a desire for justice. Nevertheless it is not wrong to be afraid of Germany's unjust encroachments and to make war in order to stop them, so long as we feared them because they attacked a just settlement and endangered our just interests. But what is the evidence? After the last war, we made the treaty of Versailles, now condemned by every one. But we have made no attempt to rectify it, even when it became urgently necessary that we should do so. We have not tried to make a just and reasonable settlement with Germany; we have merely allowed Germany to set aside portions of the treaty by force, and with grave injustice. Finally, we have clamoured to negotiate at the last moment, when otherwise Germany would take by force; and our offers have been rejected. Unjustly, it may be; but the evil done by our enemies does not affect our own condemnation.

Our policy, it might be said, is incomprehensible, except as a policy, not of opposing German injustice, but of trying to preserve the status quo and that an unjust one. Some of us may think the case clear enough; yet such argument is likely to lead us into endless controversy. It may be that we could not prove irrefutably that our government's aims are positively vicious.

Some might say that the government is not clear enough about its aims for them to be vicious. Yet if this is so, the government's intention in fighting the war must still be condemned. For it is a condition of a just war that it *should* be fought with a *just* intention; not that it should *not* be fought with an *unjust* intention. If the government's intentions cannot be known to be unjust because they are vague, that vagueness itself vitiates them. But the case is even clearer than this. For the truth is that the government's professed intentions are not merely vague, but unlimited. They have not said: "When justice is done on points A, B and C, then we will stop fighting." They have talked about "sweeping away everything that Hitlerism stands for" and about "building a new order in Europe". What does this mean but that our intentions are so unlimited that there is no point at which we or the Germans could say to our government: "Stop fighting; for your conditions are satisfied." It is true that our government has said that it will not consider peace negotiations until certain injustices are set right. But it has made this only a necessary and not a sufficient condition; therefore it is nothing against our argument.

There results a tendency to interpret our government's phrases according to various predilections. A socialist will tell you that he is fighting for social justice and free speech, a Catholic that he is fighting for the Church. We should forget our own desires and consider narrowly what can be deduced from our government's actions, coupled with these vague and inevitable catchwords. There can be only one conclusion: we are fighting against an unjust cause, indeed; but not for a just one.

5 *On the Morality of Means*

Before considering whether or not there are any persons who may not be attacked in war, we must try to elucidate, in however crude a fashion, the doctrine of intention in human acts. For in all actions of rational beings we can distinguish three ends of action: there is the motive or motives of the agent, the proper effect of the act as such, and the completed act itself. These are not always distinct in fact, but they can be; if they do coincide this does not make them less distinct in nature, though the distinction is sometimes subtle. For example, take the action of a carpenter in the stroke of a chisel. His motive may be the glory of God, or the obtaining of wages, or the satisfaction of a completed job, or several or all of these, and more besides. The proper effect of the act as such is the removal of a shaving of wood, and this may also be considered as one of the ends of the agent as well as of the action. The completed act itself is simply the completed successful stroke. Let us apply this analysis to military attack. The motive may be to win the war, or medals, or simply to attack successfully and destroy the enemy who receive the impact of the attack. The proper effect is the weakening, disabling or destruction of those who receive that impact. The completed act itself is the completed attack, or, in the case, let us say, of bombing, the dropping and explosion in the right place of the bomb.

Now as to morals. If an act is to be lawful, it is not sufficient that the motives of the agent should be good, though this is necessary. First, the act itself must not be intrinsically wrong; it must not be such an act as is wrong under any circumstance. Second, the proper effects of the act must be permissible. And unless these conditions are present, the act is wrong. To apply these principles once more in the case of military attack: an attack on men is not intrinsically vicious: is not, that is, a perverted act; it is circumstances that make it right or wrong. The motive of the attackers belongs to a consideration of aims rather than of means; or, if we are considering individual soldiers, it is matter for God at the Last Judgement, not for us here. But what of the proper effects of the completed action? These, as we have seen, consist in the destruction of the persons attacked. If, therefore, the attack is to be lawful, the persons attacked must be persons whom the attackers may legitimately destroy. Our object is to consider whether in warfare these persons include civilians.

6   On Means

(i) *The prospect of attack on civilians:* It is generally recognized that, in certain circumstances, we shall attack civilians from the air; we are already attacking them by blockade. We have no space to prove these facts in detail: for the first, it suffices to recall the answer made by our government to President Roosevelt, when he asked for a promise not to attack civilians. We said that we should adhere to international law on the matter, but that we reserved the right "to adopt appropriate measures" if the Germans should break it. If the right to adopt appropriate measures is a reservation to a promise not to attack civilians, then it can only mean that, given certain circumstances, we should attack civilians. The language is veiled, but it can hardly be interpreted in any other way.

(ii) *On blockade:* As for blockade: it has been pretended, in justification, that the blockade is not a blockade; or that it does not attack civilians. But some people, when they are arguing on another subject, when they are assuring us of victory, *then* they tell us that we cannot but win because the Germans cannot survive the blockade, since it prevents things essential to their national life from reaching them. Others, at this point, say that we could not really be responsible for starving the German people, because they divert the supplies to the fighting forces, and therefore are responsible themselves. But this argument admits that civilians do suffer attack and therefore can be dealt with under that head.

(iii) *The 'indivisibility' of modern war and the justification of killing enemies in war.* It is argued that it is just to attack civilians in war because war is now "indivisible". The civilian population is really as much combatant as the fighting forces, for it is their essential backing. The military strength of a country is its whole economic and social strength. Therefore civilians may be attacked as combatants.

Here we must ask two questions: first, what is the justification of killing in war? and, second, in what does the indivisibility of war consist? It is no sin to kill a man in self-defence or in defence of rights, if there is no possibility of appeal to a higher authority. A private person can appeal to the authority of the state, and therefore has no right to choose the death of a man in order to defend his rights; though he commits no sin if his action in resisting attack, at the time of attack, results in the death of the attacker; for such death is accidental. But where there is no higher authority to which to appeal, as in the case of a sovereign state at war, men who are wrongfully attacking rights may be killed in order to defend those rights if they cannot be defended in any other way.

We must notice two things about this doctrine: first that those who are killed are killed as *wrongfully* attacking rights, in virtue of the fact that it is not possible to appeal to any higher authority than the parties in the dispute. In this sense, the justly warring state is 'in the stead of a judge', having chosen to inflict death on men for the general good. Those men *must* be *wrongfully attacking* rights, or retaining what they have *wrongfully* gained; for it is wrong to slay the innocent for the good of the people. But second, though it proceeds from this quasi-judicial position of the justly warring state, that it can give its ministers authority deliberately to kill its enemies, *yet* they may only kill as a means of self-defence or the defence of rights; the judicial power does not permit them to kill purely punitively; for it is not lawful to kill men simply punitively, except after trial. The justly warring state has to judge of the right or wrong done; but it has no power of judgement on personal guilt or innocence. These two points must therefore be maintained: to quote St Thomas Aquinas,

> it is unlawful for a man to intend to kill any one in order to defend himself, except for one with public authority; and he, intending to kill a man for his own defence, refers this to the general good, as is plain in the case of a soldier fighting enemies, and the minister of a judge fighting against robbers. (2a 2ae. 64, art. 7.)

We have it, then, that no one may be deliberately attacked in war, unless his actions constitute an attack on the rights which are being defended or restored. To deny this will be to assert that we may attack any one anywhere, whose life in any way hinders the prosecution of the war, or in any way assists our enemies; and such a conclusion is as immoral as to be a *reductio ad absurdum* in itself.

Now in what does the 'indivisibility' of war consist? It consists in this, that it would be impossible for the combatant forces to fight, unless they were backed by the economic and social strength of the nation behind them. Therefore, it is argued, the civil population is a military target. To this there is only one reply. The civilian population behind an army does not fulfil the conditions which make it right to kill a man in war. Civilians are not committing wrong acts against those who are defending or restoring rights. They are maintaining the economic and social strength of a nation, and that is not wrong, even though that strength is being used by their government as the essential backing of an army unjustly fighting in the field.

It has been argued that, as accessories to a murder are by law punished equally with the murderer, so the citizens of an enemy country may be killed equally with the fighting forces. But the analogy is false. An accessory is punished as morally guilty of murder. But we have seen that it is not right to kill merely punitively in war; so whatever the guilt of the enemy nation, we cannot arrogate to ourselves the position of a judge, and execute them. A man cannot be judge in his own suit; and we are one of the parties in the quarrel. In default of a higher authority, we may kill those whose actions are an attack on our rights, in order to defend those rights: but the actions must themselves be wrong. The actions of a great mass of the civilian population are not in themselves wrongful attacks on us. Therefore they may not be killed by us, simply as deserving to die, nor yet because their death would be useful to us.

(iv) *A note on reprisals:* It follows from this analysis that no warring state may claim the right to reprisals as such, because the other side deserves them. It is not right to inflict a certain harm on the enemy simply because he has inflicted it on you.[4] The morality of the action itself must be considered before it can be justified.

(v) *On double effect:* It has been argued that it is justifiable to attack civilians because their death is an example of "double effect". But this is no example of double effect, which is exemplified when an action designed to produce one effect produces another as well by accident. If, for example, a military target is being attacked and in the course of the attack civilians are also destroyed, then their destruction is not wicked, for it is accidental. Obviously before their destruction can be passed over on these grounds, it must also be shown that the action is of sufficient importance to allow such grave incidental effects. No action can be excused whose consequences involve a greater evil than the good of the action itself, whether these consequences are accidental or not.[5] Double effect therefore only excuses a grave incidental consequence where the balance of the total effects of an action is on the side of the good.

There is a great distinction between attacking a group of persons directly, and killing them accidentally in the course of attack on others. But yet

---

[4] This, of course, does not apply to denunciation of those parts of international law not affected by the natural law.

[5] Ctr. Thomas Aquinas, *Summa Theologica* 2a 2ae. 64, *De Homicidio*, on the example of killing in self-defence. "The force used must be proportioned to the necessity."

another distinction must be made. It is a different thing, while making one group of persons a target, to kill others by accident, and to make a group of persons a target, in order – by attacking them all – to attack some members of the group who are persons who may legitimately be attacked. The first case involves no sin; the second involves murder and is not an example of double effect. It has been claimed as such by some who, defending blockade, allow that civilians are not a proper military target, but who argue that attack may be made on a whole group of persons which includes both civilians and combatants. This claim cannot be allowed.

Again, we cannot say with regard to blockade that the starvation of a civilian population by the diversion of supplies to its army is an incidental and unintentional effect of an action intended to demoralize the army. For to do so it would be necessary not only to prove that such an evil effect would in fact be outweighed by the good effects expected, but also that there would be no causal relation between the preceding starvation of a civilian population and the demoralization of an army.[6] This aspect of the problem of double effect is distinct from that treated immediately above. There we were considering whether it is an example of double effect to attack one group of persons as a means of destroying a part of the same group; here, whether an alleged example of double effect is not rather an attack on one group of persons as a means to attacking another and distinct group. Both cases are immoral if a group of, or including, civilians, is made a military target; and neither is a case of double effect.

(vi) *On the balance of good and evil:* It is said that war admittedly produces a number of evil effects, including attacks on civilians, but that these must be balanced against the probable good effects of the war, and if they are outweighed by good, then they can be discounted. It is indeed true that such a balance must be made; but we cannot propose to sin, because that evil will be outweighed by the good effects of the war. That would be to commit sin that good might come; and we may not commit any sin, however small, for the sake of any good, however great, and if the choice lies between our total destruction and the commission of sin, then we must choose to be destroyed.

There is a sense in which it is true to say that the sinful means chosen by the government would not vitiate the whole of a war, on account of the smallness of the sin. Though we could not join in committing the sin, however small, yet if it were very small, it would not, on account of the 'parvity of matter' render the whole war wrong. But unjust deliberate killing is murder and this is a great sin which 'cries to heaven for vengeance'; if, therefore, the warring state intends, under any circumstances, to commit it as a means of prosecuting the war, then the war is made wicked. As we have seen, our government does intend to do that which is unlawful, and it is already blockading Germany with intent to starve the national life. The present war is therefore wrong on account of means.

[6] See any textbook of moral theology.

(vii) *On propaganda:* Europe since the outbreak of war has been comparatively quiet, and in consequence indiscriminate hatred has been far less noticeable than it was during the last war. But as the conflict grows more serious, we cannot expect this state of things to last; already there is less moderation in public speeches and private conversation than at the outset. Worse, there is already suppression and distortion of truth 'in the interests of the state'; and news has become propaganda and advocacy of a case. One man's lies are not justified because they contradict another's. We assert that, on the contrary, to fight for, while not observing, truth, is the same contradiction, madness and unreason which we condemn among the Nazis.

7   On the Probable Evil Effects of the War

Finally it remains to consider the last condition. The probable good effects of a war must outweigh its probable evil ones. We hold to the contrary that in this present struggle this condition is not satisfied. We have seen that our government's aims are suspect at the outset; that it is fighting with no desire for justice, so far as we can see, and that it is either ignorant of morals or malicious as far as means are concerned. What is likely to be the end, if we win, if this is what we are like at the beginning? To quote Pope Pius XII in his first encyclical:

> Let us leave the past and turn our eyes to the future which according to those who control the fate and fortune of the peoples, is to consist, once the bloody conflicts have ceased, in a new order, founded on justice and prosperity. Will that future really be different: above all, will it really be better? Will the treaties of peace, will the new international order at the end of the war be animated by justice and equity towards all, by that spirit which frees and pacifies? Or will there be a lamentable repetition of the ancient and recent errors? To hope for a decisive change exclusively from the shock of war and its final issue is idle, as experience shows. The hour of victory is the hour of external triumph for the party to whom the victory falls, but it is, in equal measure, the hour of temptation. In this hour the angel of justice strives with the demon of violence . . . the excited passions of the people, often inflamed by the sacrifices and sufferings they have borne, obscure the vision, even of responsible persons, and make them inattentive to the warning voice of humanity and equity which is overwhelmed and drowned in the inhuman cry 'woe to the conquered'. There is danger lest settlements and decisions born under such conditions be nothing else than injustice under the cloak of justice.[7]

If, therefore, there is little chance of a just and lasting peace, of a "new order in Europe", do not all the inevitable evils which accompany war also condemn this one?

It has been said that the victory of the Allies would at least be better than

---

[7] *Summi Pontificatus*, pages 29–30, in the Vatican Latin edition. When quoting from this encyclical we have sometimes made use of the Vatican official English translation, sometimes of the English version of Mgr Knox; but comparing these with the Latin original we have often found cause to alter the translation ourselves.

that of their enemies; for there would be a certain fluidity in the situation which we could scarcely expect if the Germans won. We must repeat that this in itself would supply no justification for the war. And the argument is fallacious. On the one hand no situation is purely static; on the other, a repeated Versailles would determine the future as inevitably and as evilly as the first. The 'preservation of democracy', the possibility of free speech, and the other such ideals which are valuable only as means, cannot weigh against considerations which belong to the essence of the moral law. The death of men, the curtailment of liberty, the destruction of property, the diminution of culture, the obscuring of judgement by passion and interest, the neglect of truth and charity, the decrease in belief and in the practice of religion – all these are the normal accompaniments of a war. We have, as we have seen, little enough hope of a just settlement to set against such prospects. And finally, there is a widespread tendency to make what our country chooses to do, the criterion of what may be done, and to call this patriotism. So a war against totalitarianism produces a totalitarian tendency; not only are morals lowered, but the very theory of morals is corrupted. If a war lasts a short while, the evils may be slight; but if the war should be engaged in for a long time with a bloody seriousness, then those evil effects will be enormous. Already men are talking of Germany as a pariah nation; they are already saying that she must henceforward be kept down and never allowed to become powerful again. And if they speak thus in England, is it not obvious that our French allies will be even fiercer in this insane determination, which is as foolish as it is immoral? Then after the war, what prospects have we, but of greater poverty, greater difficulties, greater misery than ever, for a space; until just another such war will break out.

Such are the probable evil effects; and they greatly outweigh the good effects of putting an end to the injustices of Germany at the present day, since we have so little hope of substituting anything for them but other injustices.

9   You Can have Sex without Children

Christianity and the New Offer

Possibility is the destruction of contentment. The necessities of the past were accepted as man's lot – or woman's lot. Women, desiring men, were more or less under their thumbs, particularly in sexual matters. Hence: very frequent childbirth, with nothing much to do about it. Any complaint was a complaint against the nature of things. Anybody's lot is hard in the absence of health, of fairness and kindness, or of prosperity and respect; for a woman, the absence of all these would be a frequent feature of her married state itself. Yet being unmarried seemed even worse – if we leave aside the monastic ideal, which provided an alternative in two religions.

But why use the past tense? This *is* the general situation; whether it is to be changed by modern technology, who can say? Yet the change now under way among the prosperous in the West is a fantastic one. The possibility of controlling conception is placed in the woman's hands, and she can still keep her man! Limitation always was possible on the man's part if he were anxious enough to avoid conception but still wanted intercourse; but the method was unpleasing and of ill-repute. Indeed many women have thus been denied children they wanted; but upon the whole such male anxiety could not be counted on to prevent women from conceiving and bearing unwillingly, in sorrow. A woman would have recourse to abortion – as little liked, but more desperately felt to be necessary.

"She must marry if she will," says St Paul, "but I think she will have trouble in the flesh." "Not nearly so much as before," says modern technology: "you can have sex without children, as much as you – or your husband – may want." What a huge difference this makes to women, and through them to society! The former situation, though still general, appears more and more intolerable. And women come more and more into consideration on their own account.

Of course things did not and do not always go so harshly; I am speaking rather of what is often actual and always a risk. Things were generally happiest in times and places where child-bearing was a woman's pride and many children her honour. Perhaps there are no such places now; according to report, abortion is everywhere very common.

We have to consider what behaviour to think right for Christians in the new situation. Till very recently the Catholic Church has taken a stand against programmes for large-scale teaching of contraceptive methods. But if it is indeed true that abortion in our time is pandemic, then this stand

From *Renewal of Religious Structures: Proceedings of the Canadian Centenary Theological Congress* (Toronto, 1968).

ought not to be kept up.[1] Even if we assume that the Church will continue the old teaching that a faithful Catholic is not to practise contraception of any kind, even so it may be desirable to have contraceptive programmes as we have brothels – to avoid worse evils; for even if contraception is bad, abortion is far worse. At one time abortion must have been increased, not decreased, by the encouragement of contraception; but in many places, if report is trustworthy, that time is past. So our view on this question is not necessarily determined by our view on the possibility of modifying the sexual code for individuals.

Possibility has turned what was once (and in general still is) perforce accepted as woman's lot into an unacceptable, because avoidable, strain and strait in her life.

But we must remember we are still the same people. If many conceptions have been and still are deplorable, then the consent to the drive that produced them was too; and it is the same drive that operates even now and is as little reflected upon.

Or should we say no? No doubt the sexual drive as such is still the same; but in the new situation, where there is contraception, are not the act and will different? Surely we must grant that there is a difference. In the old situation, there was a will and an act contrary to the virtue of chastity because of the reckless and callous begetting of children; surely now there is a significant difference, if improvident procreation is excluded? I think it is easier to see what we must say here than to give an account of the answer.

The great change in the world means that there must be a great change in the attitudes and thoughts of the great mass of believing and practising lay people. For centuries past, the laity could be passive, except for the rare individual and except for each one's secret spiritual life. The reason was the existence of 'Christendom'. Under Christendom, it no longer took special energy to be a Christian, as in the early centuries; in most places in Christian countries, people did not have to choose a form of life. There just was a basic form of life there: lay people – especially laywomen – either were its victims or, favoured by fortune, were happy in it. Goodness or badness of life was a specification *within* the basic form. Someone who wanted to lead a holy life would often, if the thought came to him in time, not marry but enter religion – decisively adopting a new form of life. A married lay person who wanted to lead a holy life would accept as from God's hand what came his, or her, way – the "trouble in the flesh" that St Paul speaks of. Numerous and burdensome pregnancies, for example, would be accepted, not at all because a distinctly ascetical form of life was being embraced; for the avoidance of them was a peculiar wickedness, and this was a woman's usual lot anyhow. Her personal goodness would develop partly in her attitude to what happened to her. Her unconditional attachment to God would then appear especially in her submission to what happened and her concern for the education of her children. The general form of Christian life more or less taught everyone the

---

[1] I came to think otherwise in the next few years. See the Introduction to this volume.

ideal of behaviour, and people more or less – no doubt rather less – con-
formed to it. An attitude towards the control of some of life's fundamental
conditions did not need to be taught, for no such control was possible. The
death of self-will – an ascetical aim – might be accomplished by a certain
manner of accepting events ordinarily unavoidable.

Now all that is changed. We need, as hardly ever before, a special energy
and a positive ascetical theology, for lay people as such. I believe we have not
yet got such a theology: can we see at all what it would be like?

We cannot see the road before us unless we can tell what to think about the
Church's teaching, so far unrevoked, on contraception – or at least what
is here at stake. That teaching might remain unrevoked, and unamended –
and unrepeated. For most people it would then become a dead letter, like the
teaching of popes, councils and all the great doctors against usury. What
confessor would now refuse absolution to me if I would not give up the
money-spinning profession of a money-lender to poor people in distress, or
would not restore interest taken for profit's sake on a personal loan to a
friend in need? But again, have you ever heard a preacher telling you that
what you have beyond the needs of your station is *owed as a debt of justice* to
relieve the needy? Yet this is Christian doctrine, and if it is not taught, the
watchmen are neglecting their office. So the teaching on contraception that
has hitherto prevailed would not turn out to have been wrong merely
because it passed into abeyance. There would rather be needed a new papal
statement, which would have to be more authoritative in form than previous
utterances to the contrary effect, and would have to explain those away. All
the same, if the doctrine did pass into abeyance this would be a very significant development; far more so than what has happened about usury; for it
would directly affect the lives of so many million lay people – *merely by default*.

So let us look at the traditional teaching. What it requires married
Catholics to endure have come to appear, in the ethos of our time, intolerable hardships. Even to *risk* these burdens now seems unacceptable,
because the risk is avoidable. The risk might come to nothing, and what in
advance looked so dreadful might prove tolerable, even happy. But if you
accept the teaching then you accept the risk and then endure what comes
even if it is very hard. For the teaching is: you turn copulation into a wrong
and shameful act if before or during or after the act you do something that
you suppose destroys the possibility of conception and do this in order to
destroy that possibility.

It is clear enough *what* is supposed to be wrong and shameful here. But in
expounding this idea people have run into difficulties: have set it forth
poorly, and on poor grounds, and surrounded with irrelevant complications.

The ground for counting such an act wrong and shameful was formerly
that it was not an act of natural intercourse. Following St Thomas, one might
define as "sins against nature" complete sexual acts which deviate from
complete acts of ordinary intercourse: these latter are acts intrinsically apt for

generation. If someone tried to avoid conception by using a *vas indebitum* in copulation, the act would obviously fall under St Thomas's definition; and the typical male contraceptive methods can also be seen to have a like character. But there are several female contraceptive methods which are different; here, the acts remain intrinsically apt for generation, physically speaking, and are made not to be apt for it only by incidental circumstances.

I must here explain a little further these concepts of an act's intrinsic character and of the character it has by incidental circumstances. In order to be an intrinsically generative *sort* of act, an act need not *itself* be actually generative; any more than an acorn needs to produce an actual oak tree in order to be an acorn. (In fact most acorns never produce oaks, and most copulations produce no offspring.) When we characterize something as an acorn we are looking to a wider context than can be seen in the acorn itself. Acorns come from oaks, and oaks come from acorns; an acorn is thus *as such generative* (of an oak), whether or not it does generate an oak; this is still true if it is planted in infertile ground or left on a shelf so that it cannot develop into an oak tree. In the same way, we may say that eating is intrinsically nutritive, the eye as such an organ of sight; consider how we would identify eating or the eye from one species to another. And it is in this sense that copulation is intrinsically generative – though there are very many copulations which in fact do not generate.

Now no theologian would have condemned copulations in which a woman found herself by process of nature in such a condition as *female* contraceptive procedures produce by art; for such copulations would still have been intrinsically of a generative type, although by further circumstance the semen would perish fruitlessly. On the other hand, whatever contraceptive devices are used, the intention in contraceptive intercourse seems to be the same, and it seems ridiculous to draw a line between methods unless indeed the sexual act itself is very deviant in kind.

We may think that some sex acts are to be excluded whatever the intention, but just for that reason it is not for anti-conceptional intent that they are excluded. The kind of acts I mean is indeed definable by this characteristic: their immediate pattern as human sexual acts is *as such* non-procreative. But if acts *not* of an inherently non-procreative kind are non-procreative in virtue of further circumstances, then surely *only* the anti-conceptional intent could be objectionable; and this in itself is *not* regarded as vitiating acts of intercourse, if use of the 'safe period' is permitted.

If this line of thought is carried further, individual acts of contraceptive intercourse will not be objectionable, unless indeed they can be characterized as acts of unnatural vice. Such a characterization becomes more and more forced as we progress through the various methods up to the pill. And there may be further developments: it could be that in the future infertility could be secured by keeping certain chemical substances out of one's diet!

Should we not therefore cease to speak of sins against nature, if we are

concerned with the ordinary copulations of married people? We may feel
that this talk does not make sense; that somehow in this century theologians
had painted themselves into a corner like an imprudent house decorator.
But in teaching that people may use infertile periods to avoid conception,
the Church is allowing what would formerly have been condemned; the
austere and grudging attitude of older authors towards sex has already been
abandoned in the modern Church. Thus, though it would indeed be a
development of teaching to allow artificial contraception, it is arguable that
what is central to that development has already taken its place in the
Church's teaching and practice. We can no longer judge by the former standards; we must rather consider such things as motives, attitudes, objectives,
and the general role of sexuality in people's lives.

I have sketched this contention; but I think, and shall try to show, that it is
philosophically incorrect. The old general position of the moral theologians
is, I think, coherent enough: only it is badly presented, without a true
rationale. The difficulty for the old position arose, as we saw, from the
following question: how can procedures be bad if they render copulation
non-generative only by a change of the circumstances surrounding an act intrinsically generative in kind? And this question splits up into two: what
characteristic of artificially contraceptive sexual acts was supposed to be condemnable? and: what makes this characteristic a condemnable one?

The answer to the first question is: *considered as intentional actions*, artificially
contraceptive acts of intercourse *are* intrinsically unapt for generation. It is
true that *just considered physically* they may be acts of an intrinsically generative
type; but since the physical circumstances that make the acts in the concrete
case non-generative, are produced on purpose by the agent so that they may
be non-generative, they cannot be considered intrinsically generative *as intentional actions*.

The point I am making here is a general one about act and intention. We
always need to distinguish the intention *embodied in* an action from the
further intentions *with* which the action is done; I am here concerned only
with the former. Whatever ulterior intentions you may or may not have, the
question first arises: what intention is inherent in the action you are actually
performing? It is one thing to have or not have certain further intentions,
another to modify the intentional action you in fact perform. What concerns
us is the question: what are you here and now doing on purpose – whatever
your ulterior aims?

Acts that are pretty clearly defined biological events, like eating and
copulation, may be said to be by nature actions of a certain kind. Eating is a
useful example to illustrate further the concepts I am using; it is a biological
example like copulation, but on the other hand we shall not here be
confused by controverted moral judgements. Eating is intrinsically a
nutritive act, the sort of act to be nutritive; this would be an essential mark of
eating if we wished to identify it in an animal species differing very much
from us in structure. Now suppose there is a state of the body in which eating

happens to be non-nutritive. (There could of course be acts of eating which, considered in a purely physical way, are *intrinsically* non-nutritive: for example, eating by a severed head kept artificially alive, with the food coming out at the neck.) If someone eats (intentionally or otherwise) at a time when his body happens to be in such a state as prevents nutrition, he is still performing what is intrinsically a nutritive act. But if he purposely brings his body into a nutrition-preventing state, then (1) his *physical act* is intrinsically a nutritive type of act and is only in the circumstances incidentally non-nutritive, but (2) his *intentional action* is intrinsically an action of non-nutritive eating.

All this gives a close analogy to generation and contraception, and should make clear the contrast between type of physical act and type of intentional action. But it would be a mistake to think that eating which is intrinsically non-nutritive (whether in its physical or in its intentional character) is as such a sin against a divinely established order of nature. And the analogous account of what makes contraception wrong is surely just as mistaken.

Disturbance of the order of nature may or may not be licit. I have no time to go into this – I shall just give a few unargued examples. To render a man's eating non-nutritive for a day or two; to install a substitute for lung-breathing by some reversible operation (with a view to underwater exploration, say); these are unobjectionable interferences with the order of nature. But it is illicit to arrange for conception independent of sexual congress, or to breed two-headed men by some surgery on the embryo. Is it licit to transplant an embryo from its mother's womb to another? Suppose this were possible, and were a means of saving a life? This is clearly a wide field of inquiry, which may become alarmingly practical. But, happily, this is not my topic.

I have tried to show that we can set up concepts of act and intentional action which make coherent sense of the line drawn by Catholic theologians between permissible and impermissible sexual actions. But granted that the line can be drawn, why should actions on one side of it be counted permissible and actions on the other side impermissible? Why was the individual sex act, in abstraction from its motive and its place in a pair of lives, reckoned to have any moral significance at all? Everybody will admit that the story does not *end* here – motive and pattern of life are important – but why does it *begin* here? Why, in short, is copulation *not* like eating – as everyone knows it is not?

It is anyhow always important to be clear what sort of intentional act one is performing. Whatever ulterior considerations there may be, I must be doing a sort of intentional act that is acceptable or excusable if I am not to be blameworthy.

But whether an individual act of eating is (say) a piece of greedy behaviour depends entirely on circumstance: and casual eating is harmless – you see a mushroom in a meadow as you walk by, and you pick and eat it without shame or shamelessness.

There is a deep association between sex and shame. No one will deny this: some may think it culture-bound, and that we should try to get away from it. But it is bound to too many cultures for that to be credible.

This shame is not a mark of any sort of disgracefulness. It is there in such bashfulness as especially exists between new lovers, new to sexual love, however innocent their union. This bashfulness shows that what is in question is not just the hiddenness of great intimacy – for bashfulness is between the pair.

This shame in our consciousness shows its face to the world partly in a characteristic mask, in sex being the subject of laughter.

This is a mysterious matter: I assume that it stems from the fall. Shame is a matter of nature, not of culture or personal fault: but surely, of flawed nature. It is not merely that individuals springing from a tainted stock have this or that tendency to evil doing which we may see in the state of the world, or in our own hearts; but also, the acts concerned with the stock itself bring shame. For no cause at all, seemingly; ought not shame to be connected only with what is shameful, disgraceful? But it occurs, as it were senselessly; yet flout it, and you get the shameless. This does not show that there was reason for the shame after all, but only that the reasonless shame has to be respected.

In any sexual activity that is wrong and pursued for its own sake, shamelessness gives the sin the peculiar flavour of lasciviousness (we may recall that the Cambridge philosopher Moore, in his *Principia Ethica*, counted lasciviousness along with cruelty as self-evidently a great intrinsic evil). Not all sexual sin has this flavour; people who in romantic love act irresponsibly and passionately and lose self-control are not properly called lascivious; this is the attractiveness of romantic love, even if it flouts wisdom and justice – sensuality is only round the corner, not yet in command.

But sensuality *is* in command in wrongful sexual actions such as almost everybody commits who lives through his or her prime: and there may be such acts even within marriage, though the blame may be small. And here we come up against a doctrine that has been constantly taught: the copulation of married couples 'purely for pleasure' is a sin against chastity, though the least of such sins. What does "purely for pleasure" mean? Obviously a couple who are aiming at getting a child do not copulate 'purely for pleasure'; but suppose they are rendering the marriage debt? Intercourse is a normal part of married life; and the most usual intent is simply to perform the act, with no further aims in view. If there is nothing against an act so performed, it will be a rendering of the debt; but such acts will take place when sensual desire prompts; and sensual desire is for intercourse as pleasurable. The vague way people formerly wrote might suggest that intercourse thus prompted by sensual desire was 'purely for pleasure', and so at least venially sinful. Rightly or wrongly ascribed to St Augustine, the view would be that when 'the debt' is rendered and a child is not aimed at, at least one partner is a bit sinful – the one whose desire sets things going in the first place.

This view we repudiate; there has clearly here been an at least inchoate development of doctrine in morals. The view suggests that the only virtuous state of mind is an unwillingness to respond to any feelings of sensual desire in oneself unless one is hoping for a child – even then, one should respond only to the extent that is necessary to perform the act. But we ought rather to say that an act of intercourse occurring as part of married life is an exercise of the virtue of chastity unless something prevents it from being so.

Catholic tradition, even at its most "gloomy, bigoted, and ferocious", has never taught that copulation is a bad kind of act: as St Augustine says, how could it be when it is the source of human society? But neither is it traditional or in itself reasonable, to regard copulation as an indifferent kind of action, like picking up a stone. Rather, copulation, like eating, is of itself a good kind of action, since like eating it preserves human life. (Our faith, which champions human nature despite the dismal results of its corruption, arms us against the temptation to deny that sustaining human existence is of itself good.) So one individual act of eating or copulation can be bad only because there is something special about it that makes it bad: normally intercourse is morally good simply as a part of married life – it is a chaste act, and an act of the virtue of chastity in one who possesses that virtue.

A severe morality holds that intercourse is vitiated if it is done without *being required* for that preservation of human kind which makes intercourse a good *sort* of action. This view is generated out of a noble love of austerity by a faulty moral psychology. God gave us our sensitive appetite, and its arousal without our calculation is part of the working of our life. The ancient moralists were right to prescribe moderation; but given moderation, acts prompted by sensuous inclination can usually be left to accomplish what makes them good in kind, without our having to calculate how to accomplish this; in the absence of something special that makes them bad, such acts are good simply as acts of a certain kind, regardless of whether they are *individually* necessary or useful for the end that makes them a good kind of action. Regular performance of such actions in this way is normal living, the normal way of preserving human existence.

Thus intercourse elicited by spontaneous sensual desire, although this is desire for pleasure, is not therefore done 'purely for pleasure', and not therefore bad. For the act is not a blind animal response, but an act of the whole human being who may rightly and reasonably be willing to respond to sensual promptings. When that is so, the act is one governed by a reasonable mind, even if no considering or reasoning goes on at the time; and it is false to say that sensuality is in command or that the act is done purely for pleasure. St Thomas's doctrine is at this point faulty and confused. He imagines unfallen man as having had sexual desire under his control in the sense that it would arise only when man summoned it up, upon a calculation that it will now be possible and good for him to procreate. And he regards the present lack of such domination by reason, and the abeyance of reason during the sex act, as marks of fallen nature. But there is no such trouble about eating as about sex, although hunger arises spontaneously, not summoned up by reason; and St Thomas himself sometimes acknowledges that there need be nothing wrong with deliberately letting reason go into abeyance, giving over considering and calculating – or else we could never rightly choose to go to sleep! But sometimes he displays an over-narrow conception of reason in comand. A man does not need to be thinking "This is my wife, and so . . ." in order that his seeking intercourse with her may count as seeking it *because* they are married and as part of their marriage.

All the same, there is such a thing in marriage as intercourse 'purely for pleasure'; and Christian tradition as a whole condemns this. Some marks of 'being purely for pleasure' would be: immoderation in, or preoccupation with sexual pleasures; succumbing to desire against wisdom; insisting against the *serious* reluctance of the other partner (the qualification is needed because of some facts of male and female psychology). In all these cases but the last both parties may be heartily consenting.

The presence of a positive intent of not procreating when desire leads to intercourse is neither a necessary nor a sufficient condition for this form of unchastity, but must raise the suspicion of it. We should notice that the intention here under discussion is not the intention already described in describing an intentional action, but is a further intention with which the action is performed. Now it is impossible (given that one knows how uncertain the result is) to copulate with the intention of procreating in this very act; at most one can engage in intercourse over a period with the intention of procreating, if both parties are fertile so far as they know. When they know procreation is naturally impossible (during pregnancy, or late in life, or because they are certainly sterile) they cannot either intend to procreate or intend not to procreate.

A man who wanted to have intercourse without the risk of children might deliberately marry a woman past childbearing or seek out a sterile woman. No marriage law could forbid this; laws have to be clearcut and not allow loopholes, and could not therefore be framed to forbid a class of marriages defined this way by their motive (a motive that of course *need* not be there when a man marries a woman known to be incapable of childbearing). But conscience should forbid such a marriage – not every legal marriage, obviously, is morally blameless – and such a man could not have intercourse chastely unless he repented (which, as King Claudius knew, may be none too easy when you enjoy the fruits of sin). But such a man is not copulating with the intent not to procreate – for the procreation he doesn't want is known to him to be impossible. All the same, failing repentance, the marriage though valid, is on his side a concubinage.

But a marriage in which the intention is to enjoy intercourse and always avoid children is invalid, not merely unchaste like the case just considered. It would not make any difference if the method of avoidance were merely regular use of infertile times: marriage contracted on this policy with a woman whose infertile time was sharply defined would be no marriage at all. We are often told that St Augustine condemned the safe period. It is not true;

he condemned the Manichean practice of seeking to avoid children altogether, by using infertile times, contraceptives and sterilizants; and we ought to condemn this too. For a number of reasons, he never considered the use of infertile times to *limit* conceptions.

I have heard that confessors' advice to young engaged couples has recently changed; that people are no longer counselled not to marry if they have the idea of marrying and having intercourse but avoiding children for some years by reason of poverty. This change appears to me to be a corruption, if the advice now given is supposed to give a guideline that can in general be safely followed.

For a long time up till recently moral theologians were preoccupied with the question what specific kinds of action are allowable, in the sense that a man who will do them need not consider himself *ipso facto* excluded from the sacraments. No doubt the aim was to avoid driving people out of the Church. "We want to make money in such-and-such ways, take such-and-such courses of action against one another, do this and that to maintain our position in the world or keep our job: can we consider this to be no sin?" The moral theologian would see if we could. But if this is the growing point of moral theology, then moral theology is developing unhealthily; for such questions are peripheral, and only if they are seen as peripheral can they be intelligently answered. One thing central to moral theology ought to be a sound philosophy of act and intention, which would have to bring this subject matter into connection with the total orientation of a human life and with the virtuous and vicious habits of human beings. For the actions and decisions that are characteristic of a virtue need not be severally obligatory, for a man in whom they are notably lacking to be a bad man.

Again, if these questions are wrongly treated as central, then moral un-soundness results – members of the Church, both clergy and laity, will in general have been getting poor moral instruction and will thus be at best enfeebled. Moreover, now that people feel dissatisfied and attempt a more positive account of morals, they tend to become mushy.

This is why in the field of sexuality we have been given, on the one hand, a set of rules about what sorts of acts may or may not be done; on the other, a lot of slush about love and family life. What *should* be is presented either in terms of specific acts that are not sinful as such, or in a sentimental picture.

One way of looking at the Church's ethical teaching about sex might be summarized as follows: outside marriage, sexual acts are simply excluded; within marriage, spouses may always use their rights (except, for example, during illness); these rights of spouses over one another's bodies are, as St Paul teaches, equal and mutual. But this sounds dry, negative, even heartless, so we attempt something more positive in the way of praising the married state and conjugal love. "Marriage is a sacrament, symbolizing the bond of Christ and the Church, and the married state a vocation; aided by grace, the Christian pair build up their Christian life together and grow in mutual love and knowledge. Their physical union plays an integral part in their growth in sanctified love." This sounds all right, but we must ask what is meant by "love": being in love, natural conjugal affection? Either of these may be lacking or only one-sided. If a kind of love cannot be commanded, then we cannot build our moral theology of marriage on the presumption that it will be present; its not being present is sad, but this sadness exists; it is very common. We must avoid speaking and writing in the sort of indicative mood that is used in the Scout Law: "A Boy Scout is kind to animals. A Boy Scout is pure in thought, word, and deed." When I read "A Christian husband and wife grow in grace and love together", my first thought is: what if they do not? It would clear the air if we substituted for the sweetness of a rosy picture the bite of a precept: "The commandment to a Christian pair is: grow in grace and love together." Then we should be in less danger of simply taking for granted that the pleasant affection which obtains between a lucky and congenial couple is already proof that the precept has been fulfilled. Where such wonderful good fortune is present, there will be the question "Are we fulfilling this precept?", no less than for a less lucky pair. The precept, as I stated it, is a joint one; a joint precept can only be obeyed in common. So the answer may have to be no: yet then there remain the separate precepts to each, and in an irremediably unhappy marriage one ought still to love the other, though the common precept cannot be obeyed, and though he does not feel the sort of affection which cannot be commanded, and which is simply good fortune.

But for such couples what application is there for the frequent description of sexual intercourse as "justified not merely for procreation but by its part in married life, as an expression of mutual love, tenderness, affection, and respect"? Are we to infer that people who are unlucky in their married life ought to abstain from intercourse? Perhaps not: people who write in this style are not, I believe, so consequent in their thinking. Clearly there are many marriages which are imperfectly happy by reason of uncongeniality but are sustained in being by habit and loyalty to the marriage bond; sexual intercourse plays a significant part in sustaining such marriages. Teaching about marriage ought absolutely not to be irrelevant to the unhappy, and flattering to the lucky. Thus the old vindication of intercourse as "rendering the marriage debt", which many find repellent nowadays, is more realistic than they are; it makes no assumption as to the state of the affections.

But if we adopt that Pauline way of talking about equal claims, then on the face of it the cards are heavily stacked in favour of female submissiveness and husbands' freedom to copulate when they want to. This is the natural consequence of the male role in sexuality (I do not mean that sexual desire is specially male). To redress this inequality, perhaps, people rather hesitantly mix in with their praise of marriage some praise of "restraint and self-control": it is very unclear what they mean. Are restraint and self-control, on both sides, praiseworthy as freely chosen austerity? Or are they, while praiseworthy, also obligatory as a form of moderation? If both sides experience desire, is abstinence praiseworthy or not? Is it perhaps as considerateness that abstinence is praiseworthy or obligatory, so that it is not virtuous moderation when considerateness does not demand it?

It is sometimes assumed that when the 'debt' is paid this is because the other partner demands it, and that partner's motive itself cannot itself be 'paying the debt'. I think this is wrong. When St Augustine depicts holy people forsaking the flesh when procreation is no longer in view, he may be assuming (though I cannot confidently accuse him of this) that when procreation is not in view desire and pleasure *must* be the ruling motive; but I think this is false, though the motive is likely enough. For whereas Augustine's holy couple have developed a bond of charity so strong as to sustain the marriage by itself and not to need to be helped by intercourse, there are very many people, not ruled by fleshly desire, who while acknowledging and admiring this austerity and holiness could not soberly judge that they themselves had already reached such a level of charity.

If moderation and considerateness are the reasons offered for abstention from sexual intercourse, is such abstention praiseworthy at all for people who are little inclined to be sexually immoderate or inconsiderate? The air was clearer, I think, when abstinence was prescribed by special rules for certain occasions – in preparation for sacraments and at specially holy or penitential seasons. These regulations are apt to puzzle us now: they seem to express that negative attitude towards sex which we now repudiate. But the idea was surely the same one as underlies periodic fasting and abstinence from some foods: religious embrace a harder discipline, but the laity too had some discipline of temporarily going without pleasures and good things.

The vestiges of the fasting and abstinence disciplines that are still with us are trivial, and it may be good if they are swept away and the management of a Christian life is left to the individual's judgement. Certainly it would not add up to much of a Christian life if one had observed these disciplines and avoided all *species* of acts that moral theologians could not find a way of allowing; particularly if one's almsgiving were the minimum ever reckoned necessary; for one's life might all the same be full of worldliness, injustice and avarice. So it may be good if the last of these regulations disappear. But the leaven of the Spirit that always works within the Church – even if it seems not much at work in this way in the present – is bound to show itself some time in a renewed vitality of ascetical ideals and practices. What form these will take we cannot say.

For myself, I should have thought it very difficult for people to make and stick to private rules, with the sort of force New Year's resolutions have: for people who want to strengthen themselves by ascetic training periods, definite known rules appear better than hand-to-mouth attempts to embody some general idea that 'restraint and self-control' are good – perhaps in a context of anxiety about births!

If the relaxation or abandonment of regulations is seen as a lowering of the price of Christianity, it is profoundly ill-conceived. Some clergy, sensitive to modern trends, seem to have been scared into flattering us in our worldliness, our sensuality and our insistence that things must go well for us. But what may in the future become a recognized ideal is that a devout and like-minded couple should for ascetical reasons arrange to practise sexual abstinence for short periods. This plan is like a slap in the face for *l'homme moyen sensuel*, so it is not likely to be commonly adopted; but so far as I know, in spite of St Paul's authority, this is not at present commonly envisaged even as an ideal plan.

People who followed this plan would be showing that they didn't regard marriage as a licence (for some reason, the only one available) to sail on the happy sea of sex – accepting children when they are an earthly blessing – though, alas, the voyage may land you on the rocks of hardship. "But Christians don't regard marriage like that!" I shall be told. "Marriage is a vocation!" What does that mean? Marriage after all – though so often unhappy – is regarded by the world as an obviously desirable state; it is the most common form of life for mankind; then, what makes it a vocation, a special calling? Three things I suggest: absolute commitment by indissoluble vows to this person alone so long as you both live; the work essential to be done for any children there may be; and the abandonment of the claim that one's own will shall dictate which path one takes from among those that offer themselves.

There is a certain ambiguity about this last token of a matrimonial vocation. St Paul tells us, in a drily factual way, that a husband seeks to please his wife, and a wife her husband, rather than the Lord (that is why it is better not to marry). This description perfectly fits most 'successful' marriages; and if it fits, it is inappropriate to speak of such a life as a vocation – many lay people must surely feel embarrassingly flattered by the word. There is indeed perhaps this much of a title to claim to be pursuing a vocation: that we are committed to, and possibly engaged in, the work of bringing up any children we may have in Christian faith and practice. But upon the whole we enter upon marriage to please ourselves, not as people entering upon a vocation; and within the framework of the commitment and task we have, surely only for very few of us is the rule of life in a marriage that is reasonably happy anything but a pleasing of ourselves and one another. Surely this is the ground for placing marriage second to religious virginity or widowhood: that we have not set the scene with a view to prayer and contemplation and the service of God as our principal concern. This does not mean that we have chosen something bad instead of something good; and the commitment by vow and (if it comes) the task of educating children do something to justify the talk of vocation. In any event, it is a vocation to be a Christian, married or not – and this *is* called a vocation in Scripture, as marriage is not.

If we really meant that marriage as such is a vocation, then we should be counselling lots of people against it. Really entering into marriage as into a vocation would mean a firm determination that for *this* marriage it shall *not* be true that the husband seeks to please his wife, and the wife her husband, rather than to please the Lord; and one might then question whether one had this vocation, if this were the idea one had in mind – and might not *want* to get married as much as many people in the world do. For it is one good thing about the West that there are various possible ways of life, so that the unmarried do not stick out like sore thumbs. People fairly often assume that at least for a woman it is a poor thing not to get married; but we should rather propagate St Paul's warning: "Let her marry if she must, but I think she will have trouble in the flesh."

Upon the whole, Christian people neither get married with a sense of *such* a vocation nor stay unmarried because they feel the lack of it; they marry because they want to, because they must; moreover, they fear loneliness, for it is also unusual in the West for unmarried people living in the world to have much community life – the married hive off in boxes, in small family units that exclude outsiders. So people must and will marry; but that doesn't make their marriage a vocation. Having married because you must, you may well accept, as one accepts a vocation, the Christian conditions of indissoluble vows and the work of rearing a family in Christian life. St Jerome's estimate is just: this is only rye bread, as compared with the fine wheat bread of the religious life – and the dung of fornication.

It is the common vocation of any Christian, married or not, to choose to please God rather than man; but I'd rather not be told that I am pursuing this vocation when I seek the comfort and success of myself and my family. Whether I am pursuing it at all depends on whether I'm ready to give all that up immediately, as Sir Thomas More did, if it hindered the submission of my will to God's. And if, in their marriages, people are not actually giving anything up? You may be sure, even if the emergency never arises, that so-and-so loves his child more than his bank account, that he would empty his bank account for his child. But unless so-and-so already practises some asceticism about possessions, it is by no means so certain that, though it has never come to a test, he loves God more than his possessions.

This is closer to our main topic than it may appear. In Ephesians 5 St Paul condemns both lechery and *pleonexia* – greediness – as vices that shut men out from the kingdom of God; either is "a worship of idols". And Christian asceticism always relates to the use of both sex and wealth, and regards as the most perfect act the act of martyrdom in which life itself is lost.

I have tried to sketch a background view of marriage against which we may look at our unanswered question: what, if anything, is bad about acts of con- traceptive intercourse? As we saw, such acts are as intentional actions (though not necessarily as physical procedures) in themselves of a kind unapt for generation. But what is wrong about them as thus described?

St Thomas replies: the order of nature is disturbed in a matter where what is done concerns the good of the species. But suppose that in the course of caring for their bit of the species – their children – a couple "disturb the order of nature", why may they not? The point of sex is indeed the produc- tion of children, but its use is necessary for the well-being of the parents beyond what is desirable for procreation; may we not then argue that contraceptive intercourse is compatible with a chaste marriage? A parallel that might be offered is the case of property: the goods of the earth are there to supply human needs, and superfluities in what each man owns are for the relief of other people's needs, but in the normal situation it is each man's business to see to the disposal of his own superfluity and not the business of other private people to take it (*Summa Theol.*, 2a 2ae. 66, art. 7).

Against this, I think one could formulate the rationale of the old objection as follows: in contraceptive intercourse the intentional action is deliberately altered from being a generative kind of action to being an act of attaining sexual climax. This account of what the intentional act here is ought, I think, to be accepted, whether we approve of such an act or not. For it is not a question of the further purpose or intention with which the act is done – to foster the well-being of the parents, sustain their love, etc. – but of what the intentional act itself is: namely, the couple's use of one another's bodies, no longer to perform a generative type of act, but for one or both to achieve orgasm.

If it is indeed all right to do this for good ends, then it is excessively difficult to see *why* after all the act need closely resemble a normal complete act of copulation; supposing that to have been made very difficult, say by a crippling accident to the wife, why should the couple not achieve sexual climax by mutual stimulation, rather than hold themselves obliged to a heroic degree of continence?

10   Rules, Rights and Promises

I

Hume had two theses about promises: one, that a promise is 'naturally unintelligible', and the other that even if (*per impossibile*) it were 'naturally intelligible' it could not *naturally* give rise to any obligation.

I regard his discovery of *natural unintelligibility* as a great one, of wider application than he gave it. But it is also quite difficult to understand.

His own exposition of these doctrines is tied up with his philosophical psychology and metaphysics and ethics, as is made clear by the following quotation.

> If anyone dissent from this [*sc.* that promises have no force antecedent to human convention] He must give a regular proof of these two propositions, viz *that there is a peculiar act of the mind, annext to promises*; and *that consequent to the act of the mind, there arises an inclination to perform, distinct from a sense of duty*.

Those who are familiar with Hume's ethics will understand this last bit, others will not. But my interest in the subject is not exegetical. I believe that Hume did hit upon a problem of intelligibility, as indeed is attested by the large literature on the topic of promises in present day analytic philosophy, and that he was correct both in calling promises "naturally unintelligible" and in framing *two* theses – and consequently for *us* distinguishing *two* problems – one, concerning what sort of beast a promise is, and the other, concerning how, given that there is such a thing, it can generate an obligation.

Hume obviously believed that he was pointing to a contrast between promises and words for perceived objects and events. These, then, he thought to be 'naturally intelligible', and the activity of meaning in which they are employed, itself also to be so. A word evokes an image, or (presumably) an image or sensation evokes a word: the image (or sensation) is an *example* of what the word stands for. It will be the upshot of the present paper that *no* language is in Hume's sense naturally intelligible. Nor is the contrast necessary for getting hold of what he was getting hold of. He saw that a promise was not a phenomenon, and so that "promise" was not a word, for which his picture of our understanding would work at all. I shall be arguing that *no* naturalistic account of a rule, as of a promise, will work: it will follow that words and their relation to their meanings aren't 'naturally intelligible' either. For the use of words involves following rules; hence an account of language must make reference to rules. (Not merely to regularities.) This, if I can put my finger on it rightly, will show just what is

From *Mid-West Studies in Philosophy* 3 (Morris, Minnesota, 1978).

wrong with empiricism. Here I want to approach this matter by explicating Hume's insight about the two problems concerning promises.

One may fail to notice that there are two problems, because a promise *signifies* the creation or willing of an obligation. It might be thought that if you could show how there can be a sign with that signification, you would be home and dry: the obligation is generated by the giving of a sign which has that signification! Hume's clarity of mind perceived that this is not so.

We might indeed argue that it was not so, from the fact that a promise may *not* generate any obligation to perform it – a promise to do something wicked, for example. Showing this might, however, leave someone puzzled; or it may be seen as a matter of defeasibility. So a direct attack is better.

I might say "Let there be a constraint upon me to do such-and-such." *This* is a sign signifying a will to be constrained. It is clear that we could understand this, and still go on to ask "*Will* there be any such constraint?" Suppose I say "Let there be a legal obligation on me to . . ." we may ask whether one was in fact brought about – e.g. whether my lawyer, to whom perhaps I gave this instruction, effected what I asked. *If* – by my merely having pronounced *those* words in appropriate circumstances and before witnesses – there is automatically created the legal fact, then this must be by a special rule of law.

Suppose that instead of "Let there be a constraint upon me to . . ." I had said "Let there *hereby* be a constraint . . ." or "There *is* hereby a constraint . . .". We may still ask "And *was* there one?" – with, of course, the extra question : "was it thereby?" It just wouldn't be an acceptable answer to say "Of course, because she said it – it doesn't need anything but that (given the circumstances) to make it so, *and you can see that from the meaning of the words*."

What does "hereby" mean? Imagine that I write on the blackboard: "I am hereby writing on the blackboard." What I wrote would be true. Again, "Let there hereby be a constraint on me . . ." or "There is hereby a constraint . . ." *might* be an utterance that was required in order to set off a paralysing device. The difference between these two is merely that we can *see* that the proposition about the writing is true, *if* we see the writing going on, and we probably don't *hear* that the constraint is brought about by hearing the utterance. For the utterance is not itself a constraining mechanism as the writing is itself the verification of the other sentence.

Now someone will say "But *that's not what 'hereby' means* in, say, a contract!" No doubt he'd be right. But let us just notice that, *if* "hereby" *did* mean that, "I hereby lay myself under an obligation . . ." (which would be an expression *saying* that an obligation was created) would necessarily always leave the question to be answered: "And *did* he? Did the obligation *get* created?" – And this exemplifies Hume's point: we have (1) tried to imagine a *natural phenomenon* of creation, by the utterance of a sign, of the sort of constraint we call obligation; (2) understood the sign to be one whose meaning is that such an obligation is being created; and (3) seen that the question would still arise whether the obligation had actually got created, and could not be proved to have the answer "Yes" by reporting that the words had been uttered. (Just as, if a door opens when I say to it: "I hereby open you," that doesn't mean that my *saying* those words itself, in suitable circumstances, is enough to prove that the door is open.)

The natural phenomenon might not have occurred, the mechanism might not have worked. Note that this is a completely different point from the point that the mere utterance of an expression: "I promise to do such-and-such" isn't even necessarily a promise – a suitable setting is needed – and that even when it *is*, it doesn't *necessarily* generate an obligation to perform it.

So we are down to understanding this special use of "hereby". For "hereby" – *not* as in "I am hereby writing on the blackboard", etc. – is what so to speak at least implicitly enters into promises. By the way, it was absurd of Hume to write as if there had to be a special sign of promising. "I'll help you today; will you help me tomorrow?" – "Yes!" Here are promises given and received. The question is what it is for them to be *promises*. They are or contain descriptions of possible future states of affairs. They are made true by performance. But they are not mere predictions, not even merely the sort of pre-diction which is an expression of intention. And one might say: this "hereby" is something attached to that in them which goes beyond being predictions and expressions of intention.

Hume's own conclusion was "that promises have no *force* antecedent to human conventions". If this is found offensive, that will be by a mis-understanding. God himself can make no promises to man except in a human language. The regularity of the seasons, and the applicability of the rational probability calculus in matters of chance, are not divine *promises*. A spouse who has always come home at a certain hour has not *eo ipso* broken any promise (only perhaps acted inconsiderately) by suddenly and wilfully failing to do so. There is indeed such a thing as implicit contract, and there might be one in this case. But that is two-sided. Mere fostering of expecta-tions can't be making an implicit contract.

The rightness of Hume's conclusions is independent both of his psy-chology and of his theory of the foundation of morals in a peculiar 'sen-timent'.

I am not interested here in the conditions requisite for making "I will . . ." into a promise. What I am interested in is this 'hereby' aspect of promising. We have seen what the 'hereby' is *not*. Because it is not that, the significance of a promise is that it not only of itself (i.e. without a mechanism) but *by its significance* purports to *make it the case* that there is a new obligation. The promise contains (perhaps on the face of it just *is*) a future-tense descrip-tion which the giver then makes come true – or he breaks the promise. The obligation is a kind of necessity to make the description come true. But what sort of necessity is that?

We may say: the necessity is one of making the description come true – *or* being guilty of something. Of what? Of breaking a promise. And what is that? A description which someone gives and which because he has given it he must make come true or be guilty. Of what? Not just to go on running round in the circle let's try again and say: of an injustice, a wrong against the one to whom the sign, the description, was given. But what *wrong* was that? The wrong of breaking a promise . . . We are back in the circle after all. A wrong is the infringement of a right. *How* does telling someone one will do something give him a right against one? Well, it does if it's a *promise*! Let's have a sign for its being that, say "I promise", put in front of the prediction. Or, because we know that too well, let's invent one: "I blip". It's not the *prediction* by itself that it's an offence not to make come true, it's the 'blipping' of it, or its being a blip. And what is the meaning of its being a blip? That it's an offence not to make the attached description come true. But *what* offence? The offence of going contrary to a blip. It seems clear that we just haven't explained what blipping is at all. Even if we could somehow get out of the circle, we have the problem: how on earth can it be the meaning of a sign that by giving it one purports to create a necessity of doing something – a necessity whose source is the sign itself, and whose nature depends on the sign.

That is Hume's first problem, translated into philosophically neutral terms. In the next section I shall point to a solution of it, which fully justifies Hume in his own solution.

II

What we have to attend to is the use of modals. Through this, we shall find that not only promises, but also rules and rights, are essences *created* and not merely captured or expressed by the grammar of our languages.

Modals come in mutually definable related pairs, as: necessary, possible; must, need not; ought, need not, etc.; together with modal inflections of other words.

When it is said that something must be, or can't but be, sometimes this is true only if it actually *is* then; sometimes only if it is later; sometimes neither matters. For the first "It *must* be in this drawer!" is an example; for the second: "So-and-so can't but win!"; for the third "You have to move your king"; or "You can't wear that!" This is a minute selection from the extremely multifarious use of modals, only a still smaller range of which has much interested philosophy in the past. Aristotle indeed made a little noted observation that one sense of "necessary" is: "that without which some good will not be attained or some evil avoided"; and in our time there have been developments of deontic logic, which shows a consciousness of kinds of modality beyond what used to be attended to.

I want to arouse interest in one range of uses, which constitutes what I'll call "stopping modals". These are of course negative; corresponding positive ones, or the positive form into which any negative modal can be put, we may call "forcing modals". The negative gets priority; it is I think more frequent than the positive, which restricts one's action to one thing. (Just as "thou shalt nots" tend to leave you freer than "thou shalts".) If I say "You can't wear that!" and it's not, e.g., that you are too fat to get it on, that's what I call a stopping modal.

Think of the game played with very small children where several players pile their hands on top of one another. Then, if one of them doesn't pull his hand out from the bottom, you say "You have to put your hand on top"; if he pulls it out too soon you say "No, you can't pull it out yet, so-and-so has to pull his out first". "You have to" and "you can't" are at first words used by one who is making you do something (or preventing you), and they quickly become themselves instruments of getting and preventing action.

After all, once this transformation has taken place, the following is true: in such a case you are told you 'can't' do something you plainly *can*, as comes out in the fact that you sometimes *do*. At the beginning, the adults will physically stop the child from doing what they say he 'can't' do. But gradually the child learns. With one set of circumstances this business is part of the build-up of the concept of a rule; with another, of a piece of etiquette; with another of a promise; in another, of an act of sacrilege or impiety; with another of a right. It is part of human intelligence to be able to learn the responses to stopping modals without which they wouldn't exist as linguistic instruments and without which these things: rules, etiquette, rights, infringements, promises, pieties and impieties would not exist either.

A stopping modal is very often accompanied by what sounds like a reason. "You can't move that, the shelf will fall down" for example shows the 'can't' to be of the type Aristotle remarked.

Similarly if I say "You can't sit there, it's N's place" – and it's clear that this is not just a personal decision of mine on a particular occasion. Now this form: "you can't . . . , it's N's . . .", though it has other applications as well, is also the form *par excellence* in which a *right* is ascribed to N. The applications under this heading may be very various. It may be "You can't *stop* N from . . . , it's N's to . . ."; or something may be N's only here and now (as we'd say of the parking-space that he's got into), or it may be quite generally something that only N can do or have, or N and people like N in some respect; or others only if *these* do not seek to do or have the thing.

In these forms of statement the second part, "it's N's . . .", has a peculiar role. It appears to be a reason. And it *is* a 'reason' in the sense of a *logos*, a thought. But if we ask what the thought is, and for what it is a reason, we'll find that we can't explain them separately. We can't explain the "You can't" on its own; in any independent sense it is simply not true that he can't (unless 'they' physically stop him). But neither does "it's N's . . ." have its peculiar sense independent of the relation to "you can't". Of course, *once these linguistic* practices exist, we can detach the two parts from one another and "it's N's" can appear as an independent reason, e.g. a reason why one will not do something.

Let me now restrict the word "reason" (in the context of action) to something independent which someone puts forward as his reason for what he does. And let me adopt the word "logos" (I might also use "theme") for the second half of "you can't . . . because . . .", where the two halves are not independent. I shall say that there are various logos-types, and that the name of the general logos-type is an abstraction from many particular cases; a label which tells you the formal character of the stopping modal. For example, one logos-type is *a right*, and another, very general one, is: *a rule*. Thus if you say "You can't move your king, he'd be in check", "he'd be in check" gives the special logos falling under the general logos type: *a rule of a game*.

Consider the learner in chess or some other game. Of course: "You have to move your king, he's in check" is equivalent to "The rules of the game require that, in this position, you move your king." But a learner may not yet have this idea: *the rules of the game require* . . . Accepting it when told "You have to move your king, he's in check", is part of learning that very concept: 'the rules of the game require'. *Requiring* is putting some sort of necessity on you, and what can that be? All these things hang together at some early stage: learning a game, learning the very idea of such a game, acquiring the concept of 'you have to' which appears in the others' speech, grasping the idea of a rule. Nor is there a distinct meaning for "being a rule of the game" (unless the general idea has been learned from other games) which can be used to *explain* the "you have to" that comes into that learning.

Now for the parallel between rules and promises. This is obscured by the fact that a promise is essentially a sign and the necessitation arises from the giving of the sign. But the problem of necessitation is nevertheless similar. I may point to a sign which states a rule. Like a promise, it contains some sort of description. What we conceive to be the necessity of acting *so* because of a rule is indeed not generated by the rule's being uttered. But the problem is similar: just as we ask what a promise is more than a mere expression of intention, we may ask what a rule is beyond a mere regularity. In explaining this one will say, e.g., that the rule is given in a formula for acting, whose meaning is that one 'must' act *thus* in accordance with it. But even if a formula can have such a meaning, why 'must' one? Because that *is* the meaning of the rule. But what *is* a rule? And, as with promises, even if we could somehow get out of this circle, we'd still have the problem: how can a formula have such a meaning?

The problem does not seem so acute, because the rule may merely be the rule of a practice which you are at liberty to engage in or not. There is after all no necessitation, other than one of following these rules *if* you wish to engage in a practice which is partly defined by them. So it does not strike one that even this conditional necessitation is problematic.

When it comes to rules of logic, it is otherwise. Let us not speak of variant logics; that is a mere distraction. For even in a variant logic, there will always be the question whether a rule has been followed. According to the rule, you can't do *that*; perhaps you must do *this*. You can't have this *and* that, you must allow this transition. Now how can a rule *inform* you that you can't do something? A rock barrier may be a natural sign that you can't go this way; or a person can tell you you can't do something. But a rule?

These 'musts' and 'can'ts' are the most basic expression of such-and-such's being a rule; just as they are the most basic expression in learning the rules of a game, and as they are too in being taught rights and manners. But they aren't, in Hume's phrase, 'naturally intelligible'. The mark of this is the relation of interdependence between the "you can't" and the 'reason' where this is what I have called the theme or logos of the "you can't". These musts and can'ts are understood by those of normal intelligence as they are trained in the practices of reason.

Part Two

The Philosophy of Religion

11   On Transubstantiation

I

It is easiest to tell what transubstantiation is by saying this: little children should be taught about it as early as possible. Not of course using the word "transubstantiation", because it is not a little child's word. But the thing can be taught, and it is best taught at mass at the consecration, the one part where a small child should be got to fix its attention on what is going on. I mean a child that is beginning to speak, one that understands enough language to be told and to tell you things that have happened and to follow a simple story. Such a child can be taught then by whispering to it such things as: "Look! Look what the priest is doing . . . He is saying Jesus' words that change the bread into Jesus' body. Now he's lifting it up. Look! Now bow your head and say 'My Lord and my God'" and then "Look, now he's taken hold of the cup. He's saying the words that change the wine into Jesus' blood. Look up at the cup. Now bow your head and say 'We believe, we adore your precious blood, O Christ of God'."[1] This need not be disturbing to the surrounding people.

If the person who takes a young child to mass always does this (not otherwise troubling it), the child thereby learns a great deal. Afterwards, or sometimes then (if for example it asks), it can be told what the words are which the priest says and how Jesus said them at the Last Supper. How he was offering himself up to the Father, the body that was going to be crucified and the blood that was going to be shed. So he showed that on the next day, when he was crucified, his death was an offering, a sacrifice. You can tell an older child how from the beginning priests have offered sacrifices to God (and to other, false, gods too) bringing animals, the best that people had, and offering them on altars: that this was how gods were worshipped, for sacrifice is the principal sign that something is being worshipped as a god. Jesus was a priest offering himself and what he did at the Last Supper showed that that was what was happening the next day on the cross. You can tell the child how he told the Apostles to do what he did at the Last Supper, and made them priests; and that that is why his words when used by a priest have the same power as they did when he said them at the Last Supper.

The worship that we learn to give at the consecration carries with it implicitly the belief in the divinity and the resurrection of the Lord. And if we do believe in his divinity and in his resurrection then we must worship what is now there on the altar.

Thus by this sort of instruction the little child learns a great deal of the

---

[1] The cry of the Ethiopians at the consecration of the chalice.

Pamphlet published by the Catholic Truth Society (London 1974).

faith. And it learns in the best possible way: as part of an action; as concerning something going on before it; as actually unifying and connecting beliefs, which is clearer and more vivifying than being taught only later, in a classroom perhaps, that we have all these beliefs.

One might not even think of mentioning our Lord's resurrection explicitly in this connection. But it is there implicitly – for it is no part of the Catholic consciousness, no part of our way of speaking of or to our Lord, to think he only comes to be, as it were intermittently, upon our altars. No, we speak of the risen man as always a living man in heaven and say that the bread and wine are changed into him. And because he is alive and not dead, his flesh is not separated from his blood, and anyone who receives any of either, receives the whole of him. So, in learning this, children learn afresh that he is alive.

I have spoken of teaching little children, both because it is important in itself and because it is the clearest way of bringing out what "transubstantiation" means. That word was devised (first in Greek and then in Latin by translation) to insist precisely upon this: that there is a change of what is there, totally into something else. A conversion of one physical reality into another *which already exists*. So it is not a coming to be of a new substance out of the stuff of an old one, as when we have a chemical change of the matter in a retort from being one kind of substance into another. Nor is it like digestion in which what you eat turns into you. For these are both changes of matter, which can assume a variety of forms. When one says "transubstantiation" one is saying exactly what one teaches the child, in teaching it that Christ's words, by the divine power given to the priest who uses them in his place, have changed the bread so that it isn't there any more (nor the stuff of which it was made) but instead there is the body of Christ. The little child can grasp this and it is implicit in the act of worship that follows the teaching. I knew a child, close upon three years old and only then beginning to talk, but taught as I have described, who was in the free space at the back of the church when the mother went to communion. "Is he in you?" the child asked when the mother came back. "Yes," she said, and to her amazement the child prostrated itself before her. I can testify to this, for I saw it happen. I once told the story to one of those theologians who unhappily (as it seems) strive to alter and water down our faith, and he deplored it: he wished to say, and hoped that the Vatican Council would say, something that would show the child's idea to be wrong. I guessed then that the poor wretch was losing the faith and indeed so, sadly, did it turn out.

"But the thing is impossible, contradictory: it cannot be believed! It has to be only a figure of speech!" Well, indeed it cannot be really understood how it is possible. But if it is claimed it is impossible, then a definite contradiction must be pointed to, and if you believe in it, you will believe that each claim to disprove it as contradictory can be answered. For example, someone says: how can a man who is, say, six foot tall be wholly in this small space? Well, indeed not by the coincidence of his dimensions with the hole in space defined by the dimensions of the remaining appearance of bread: let us call this the 'dimensive' way of being in a place. "But that is the only way for a body to be in a place!" How do you know? We believe that something is true of *That* which is there, which contradicts its being there dimensively. And certainly the division and separation from one another of all these places where That is, does not mean a division and separation of *it* from itself. So, considered dimensively, a thousand such diverse places can be compared to a thousand pieces of mirror each of which reflects one whole body, itself much bigger than any of them and itself not dimensively displaced. But when we consider *That* which the bread has become, the place where we are looking has become (though not dimensively) the place where *it* is: a place in heaven.

It would be wrong to think, however, that the thing can be understood, sorted out, expounded as a possibility with nothing mysterious about it. That is, that it can be understood in such a way as is perhaps demanded by those who attack it on the ground of the obvious difficulties. It was perhaps a fault of the old exposition in terms of a distinction between the substance of a thing (supposed to be unascertainable) and its accidents, that this exposition was sometimes offered as if it were supposed to make everything intelligible. Greater learning would indeed remove that impression. For in the philosophy of scholastic Aristotelianism in which those distinctions were drawn, transubstantiation is as difficult, as 'impossible', as it seems to any ordinary reflection. And it is right that it should be so. When we call something a mystery, we mean that we cannot iron out the difficulties about understanding it and demonstrate once for all that it is perfectly possible. Nevertheless we do not believe that contradictions and absurdities can be true, or that anything logically demonstrable from things known can be false. And so we believe that there are answers to supposed proofs of absurdity, whether or not we are clever enough to find them.

II

Why do we do this – why do we celebrate the Eucharist? Because the Lord told us to. That is reason enough. But we can reflect that it is his way of being present with us in his physical[2] reality until the end of this age; until he comes again to be dimensively and visibly present on earth. We can also reflect on the mysterious fact that he wanted to nourish us with himself.

This to my mind is the greatest mystery of all about the Eucharistic sacrifice, a greater mystery than transubstantiation itself, though it must be an essential part of the significance of transubstantiation. To try to get some

[2] Theologians have not been accustomed to say that our Lord is 'physically' present in the Eucharist. I think this is because to them "physically" means "naturally", as the word comes from the Greek for *nature* – and of course our Lord is not present in a natural manner! But to a modern man to deny that he is physically present is to deny the doctrine of the Catholic Church – for meanings of words change. Pope Paul VI tells us in the Encyclical *Mysterium Fidei* that "Christ is present whole and entire, bodily present, in his physical reality".

understanding of this, let us first ask ourselves what our Lord was doing at the Last Supper. If you ask an orthodox Jew to say grace at your table, he will take a piece of bread in his hands, will pray and break the bread and distribute a piece to each person present. So our Lord was then saying grace – and on a special occasion. He was celebrating the Passover; this supper was the first, highly ceremonial meal of the days during which Jews celebrate the passage of the angel of the Lord over Egypt when they were about to escape from their Egyptian slavery. Then they had to sacrifice a lamb, in groups large enough to eat it up, they were to smear their doorposts with its blood; the angel of the Lord passed over their houses, destroying the first-born children of all other houses. The Jews ate their sacrifice, being commanded on this occasion to eat all up and leave nothing behind; they stood ready to go on their journey, ready to leave Egypt. This meal in preparation for the journey out of bondage has ever since been memorialized in the supper – the Seder as present-day Jews call it – which was celebrated by our Lord with his disciples. But to the grace our Lord adds the words "This is my body" and after the rest of the celebration, he takes the cup of wine and says it is "my blood which will be shed for you". We have seen how this showed that his coming death was a sacrifice of which he was the priest. (For his death was voluntary; no one could take his life from him if he would not give it up.) His actions showed that for us he himself replaced the Passover lamb, which was originally both a sacrifice and the meal in preparation for the journey of escape from slavery, and also provided the sign of difference between the escaping Jews and those who would have detained them.

There are two sorts of sacrifice, the holocaust, or 'wholeburning' in which the whole of the sacrificed victim is destroyed in the sacrifice, and the kind in which the people eat what is sacrificed.

Christ made of himself the second kind; his first command in his grace-saying was to eat; it subsequently emerges that he is making a sacrificial offering and that he is superseding the paschal lamb, assuming its place. Catholics believe that we cannot eat and drink what he commanded without having the same bread and the same cup to eat and drink of; and *that* we can only do by reproducing his own offering. This, then, is why we identify the offering of the Last Supper with the sacrifice on the cross and with every mass.

So his flesh and blood are given us for food, and this is surely a great mystery. It is clearly a symbol: we are not physically nourished by Christ's flesh and blood as the Jews were by the paschal lamb.

We Christians are so much accustomed to the idea of holy communion that we tend not to notice how mysterious an idea it is. There is the now old dispute between Catholics and Protestants whether we eat what only symbolizes, or really is, the flesh of the saviour when we eat the bread consecrated in the Eucharist; drink his blood only symbolically or really. Because of this dispute, it appeared as if only the Catholic belief were extravagant – the Protestants having the perfectly reasonable procedure of *sym-*

bolically eating Christ's flesh and drinking his blood! The staggering strangeness of doing such a thing even only symbolically slipped out of notice in the disputes about transubstantiation. But let us realize it now.

For why should anyone want to eat someone's flesh or drink his blood? "I will drink your blood" might be a vow made against an enemy. Indeed in Old Testament language eating a man's flesh and drinking his blood is an idea expressive of just such deadly enmity. Or savage peoples have wanted to eat the flesh of a brave enemy to acquire his virtue. Someone puzzled at the Christian Eucharist, whether celebrated under Catholic or Protestant conceptions, might wonder if that was the idea; but he would be far off the mark. Are Christians then like savage tribes, which on special occasions may eat the animals that are tabu at other times? No, that is not it.

It is surely clear that the reason why Christians have this sacrifice is obedience to the injunction of the saviour. He told his disciples to do this as *his* reminder (*sc.* to the Father), and said that what they ate and drank was his body and blood. And they might claim not to understand the matter, not to know any more about it than that he told them to do it and said it was a means to eternal life. I mean: it is not necessarily as it were a natural or intelligible gesture for them to make. To see this, imagine that there were a ceremony called 'kissing the feet of the saviour' or 'binding oneself to him'. These would be intelligible gestures, one would understand the thought of which they were the expression. But *eating* him?

Certainly this eating and drinking are themselves symbolic. I mean that, whether this is itself a literal or is a purely symbolical eating of his flesh and drinking of his blood, *that* is in turn symbolical of something else. So if we only symbolically (and not really) eat his flesh, our action is the symbol of a symbol. If we literally eat his flesh our action is a direct symbol. The reason why the action is in any case strange and arcane is this: it is not a natural or easily intelligible symbol. How, and what, it symbolizes – that is deeply mysterious.

In modern times some theologians have tried to explain transubstantiation as trans-signification. The 'substance' of some things is the meaning they have in human life. This is certainly true of some things, like money, and they have wished to say it is true of bread and wine: these aren't chemical substances, but mean human food and drink. Well, as to the first point (that they aren't single substances) that's true enough; but the bread and wine that are fit to use at the Eucharist are defined by the natural kinds they are made from, by wheat and grape. For the rest, what is said may be very true – but the odd thing, which apparently is not noticed, is that what gets trans-signified in the Eucharist is not the bread and wine, but the body and blood of the Lord, which are trans-signified into food and drink. And that is the mystery.

When Jesus said, "I am the bread that came down from heaven", his words were a metaphor for the same thing. The metaphor is that of saying "I myself will be the nourishment of the life of which I speak." The saying is dark, like his saying "I *am* the way", "I *am* the truth" and "I *am* the life" or again "I *am* the door". Not "My way is the way" or "I show you the truth", but "I am the way and the truth". Similarly not "I have nourishment for you" but "I am the bread". The commanded action of eating his flesh creates the very same metaphor as the words – whether we take the description of the action literally or symbolically. For, even if the words "I am the bread (i.e. the food) that came down from heaven" are to be taken literally, still that which they say, and which on *that* understanding is literally so, symbolizes something *else*.

The clearest of his metaphors is that of the vine. We can say *un*metaphorically what that says – that the life he speaks of is his own; as the life of the branches is that of the vine. So this is the teaching that disciples are not merely disciples (taught) but are to share in the divine life, the divine nature itself. But here again understanding stops. Except that if it is so, we get an inkling why he does not merely say that he shows the way, the truth, a life, and can supply what is needed for that life (as a teacher can give studies that will nourish the pupil), but that he *is* the way, is the truth, is the life. But no one can know what it means for us to live with the life of God himself. That is why I say that what is symbolized by that symbol, the eating of that flesh and drinking of that blood (whether that is done literally or in turn only in symbol) is deeply mysterious. No wonder the early Christians were accused of some weird orgy in their Eucharist, and answered only with denials that any abomination took place.

"He gives us his body", so Augustine wrote, "to make us into his body." This brings out how the sacrament symbolizes and effects the unity of the people who join together to celebrate the Eucharist and to receive communion. The 'mystical body of Christ' which we call the church, is a *body* in figure or metaphor. The unity of mankind is already spoken of in the metaphor by which we are considered to be born all 'members of Adam'. Calling this one body, as if all men constituted one big man, is of course a figure or metaphor; the unity of life that is pointed to in the metaphor is itself no metaphor, for we are all, all the races of men, of one stock and one blood. Now by baptism we are said to be grafted into the body of a new Adam, and here again we have the metaphor of being the members – which means the limbs and other bodily parts – of the body of one man. Once again, *the unity of the life that is pointed to* in the figure of speech is *no* metaphor. Of this life Christ called himself the food. It is the food of the divine life which is promised and started in us: the viaticum of our perpetual flight from Egypt which is the bondage of sin; the sacrificial offering by which we were reconciled; the sign of our unity with one another in him. It is the mystery of the faith which is the same for the simple and the learned. For they believe the same, and what is grasped by the simple is not better understood by the learned: their service is to clear away the rubbish which the human reason so often throws in the way to create obstacles.

12 Faith

In the late 1960s some sentence in a sermon would often begin: "We used to believe that . . .". I always heard this phrase with an alarmed sinking of the heart. I had alternative expectations. The more hopeful one was for some absurd lie. For example: "We used to believe that anyone was safe for Heaven if he kept the Church rules." "We used to believe that there was no worse sin than to miss mass on Sunday." The worse one was of hearing something like "We used to believe that there was something special about the priesthood;" "We used to believe that the Church was here for the salvation of souls."

Now there was a "We used to believe . . ." which I think could have been said with some truth and where the implied rejection wasn't a disaster. There was in the preceding time a professed enthusiasm for rationality, perhaps inspired by the teaching of Vatican I against fideism, certainly carried along by the promotion of neo-thomist studies. To the educated laity and the clergy trained in those days, the word was that the Catholic Christian faith was *rational*, and a problem, to those able to feel it as a problem, was how it was *gratuitous* – a special gift of grace. Why would it *essentially* need the promptings of grace to follow a process of reasoning? It was as if we were assured there was a chain of proof. First, God. Then, the divinity of Jesus Christ. Then, *his* establishment of a Church with a Pope at the head of it and with a teaching commission from him. This body was readily identifiable. Hence you could demonstrate the truth of what the Church taught. Faith, indeed, is not the same thing as knowledge – but that could be accounted for by the *extrinsic* character of the proofs of the *de fide* doctrines. The knowledge which was contrasted with faith, would be knowledge by proofs *intrinsic* to the subject matter, not by proofs from someone's having *said* these things were true. For matters which were strictly 'of faith' intrinsic proofs were not possible, and that was why faith contrasted with 'knowledge'.

This is a picture of the more extravagant form of this teaching. A more sober variation would relate to the Church that our Lord established. In this variant one wouldn't identify the church by its having the Pope, but otherwise; and one would discover that it had a Pope and that that was all right. This more sober form had the merit of allowing that the believer was committed to the Christian faith, rather than suggesting that he had as it were signed a blank cheque to be filled out by the Pope in no matter what sum.

A yet more sober variant would have avoided trading on the cultural in-

This paper has not previously been published. It was delivered as a Wiseman Lecture at Oscott College.

heritage for which the name of Jesus was so holy that it was easy to go straight from belief in God to belief in Jesus as God's Son. In this more sober variant one would be aware of the dependence of the New Testament on the Old: one would be clearly conscious of the meaning of calling our Lord "Christ".

The 'sober variants' would have a disadvantage for the propagandists of the rationality (near demonstrability) of faith – though a great advantage in respect of honesty and truthfulness. The disadvantage was that no one could suppose it quite easy for anyone to see that what Jesus established was matched by the Catholic Church that we know. If it was just a matter of his having founded a Church with a Pope, then it was easy indeed! But otherwise it was *obvious* that learning and skill would be required to make the identification. And the considerations and arguments would be multifarious and difficult to be sure about. Hence the problem most commonly felt, amongst the more intellectual enquirers, as to the character of the *certainty* ascribed to faith. The so-called preambles of faith could not possibly have the sort of certainty that *it* had. And if less, then where was the vaunted rationality?

But there was a graver problem. What about the 'faith of the simple'? They could not know all these things. Did they then have some inferior brand of faith? Surely not! And anyway, did those who studied really think *they* knew all these things? No: but the implication was that the knowledge was there somehow, perhaps scattered through different learned heads, perhaps merely theoretically and abstractly available. In the belief that this was so, one was being rational in having faith. But then it had to be acknowledged that all this was problematic – and so adherence to faith was really a matter of hanging on, and both its being a *gift* and its *voluntariness* would *at this point* be stressed.

I sometimes hear accounts of the times of darkness before Vatican II which strike me as lies. I hope that I have not been guilty of lying in what I have said here. This at least is my recollection of how it was in some presentations, some discussions, some apologetic.

Was, and is no longer, not necessarily because better thoughts about faith are now common; there is a vacuum where these ideas once were prominent. But all these considerations, proofs, arguments and problems are now out of fashion, for various reasons which I won't discuss.

The passing away of these opinions is not to be regretted. They attached the character of 'rationality' entirely to what were called the preambles and to the passage from the preambles to faith itself. But both these preambles and that passage were in fact an 'ideal' construction – and by 'ideal' I don't mean one which would have been a good development of thinking, if it had occurred in an individual; I mean rather 'fanciful', indeed dreamed up according to prejudices: prejudices, that is, about what it is to be reasonable in holding a belief.

The right designation for what are called the "preambles" of faith is not that but at least for part of them, "presuppositions". Let me explain this in a simple example. You receive a letter from soneone you know, let's call him Jones. In it, he tells you that his wife has died. You believe him. That is, you now believe that his wife has died because you believe *him*. Let us call this just what it used to be called, "human faith". That sense of "faith" still occurs in our language. "Why", someone may be asked, "do you believe such-and-such?", and he may reply "I just took it on faith – so-and-so told me".

Now this believing Jones, that his wife has died, has a number of presuppositions. In believing it *you* presuppose (1) that your friend Jones exists, (2) that this letter really is from him, (3) that that really is what the letter tells you. In ordinary circumstances, of course, none of these things is likely to be in doubt, but that makes no difference. Those three convictions or assumptions are, logically, presuppositions that *you* have if your belief that Jones' wife has died is a case of your believing Jones.

Note that I say they are *your* presuppositions. I do not say that your believing Jones entails those three things; only that your believing Jones entails that you *believe* those three things.

In modern usage "faith" tends to mean religion, or religious belief. But the concept of faith has its original home in a particular religious tradition. If a Buddhist speaks of "his faith", saying for example that his faith ought not to be insulted, he means his religion, and he is borrowing the word "faith" which is really alien to his tradition. In the tradition where that concept has its origin, "faith" is short for "divine faith" and means "believing God". And it was *so* used, among the Christian thinkers at least, that faith, in this sense, could not be anything but true. Faith was believing God, as Abraham believed God, and no false belief could be part of it.

I want to say what might be understood about faith by someone who did not have any; someone, even, who does not necessarily believe that God exists, but who is able to think carefully and truthfully about it. Bertrand Russell called faith "certainty without proof". That seems correct. Ambrose Bierce has a definition in his Devil's Dictionary: "The attitude of mind of one who believes without evidence one who tells without knowledge things without parallel". What should we think of this?

According to faith itself faith is believing God. If the presuppositions are true, it is, then, believing on the best possible grounds someone who speaks with perfect knowledge. If only the presuppositions were given, Bierce would be a silly fellow and Russell would be confuted. But is there even the possibility of 'believing God'? This is hard to grasp: it is itself one of the 'things without parallel'.

Anyway, in general, 'faith comes by hearing', that is, those who have faith *learn* what they believe by faith, learn it from other people. So someone who so believes believes what is told him by another human, who may be very ignorant of everything except that *this* is what he has to tell as the content of faith. So Bierce's Devil may be right. One who has not evidence believes one who has not knowledge (except of that one thing): at least, he believes what the latter says and he gets what he believes from the latter; yet according to faith he believes God. If so, then according to faith a simple man – a man with no knowledge of evidence – may have faith when he is taught by a man ignorant of everything except that these are the things that faith believes. More than that, according to faith this simple man and his teacher have a belief in no way inferior to that of a very learned and clever person who has faith.

If faith is like that, even if it is believing God, then it follows that the Bierce definition is right after all. For everyone is to have faith and few can be learned, and their learning doesn't give them a superior kind of faith. Everyone is to run: and few are road-sweepers.

It is clear that the topic I introduced of *believing somebody* is in the middle of our target. Let us go back to Jones, and investigate *believing Jones*, when you read in his letter that his wife has died. You can't call it believing Jones just if Jones says something or other and you do believe that very thing that he says. For you might believe it anyway. And even if it's someone's saying something that *causes* you to believe it, that doesn't have to be believing *him*. He might just be making you realize it, calling it to your attention – but you judge the matter for yourself. Nor is it even sufficient that his saying it is your *evidence* that it is true.[1] For suppose that you are convinced that he will both lie to you, i.e. say the opposite of what he really believes, and be mistaken? That is, the opposite of what he thinks will be true; and he will say the opposite of what he thinks. So what he says will be true and you will believe it because he says it. But you won't be believing him!

Ordinarily, of course, when you believe what a man says, this is because you assume that he says what he believes. But even this doesn't give us a sufficient condition for your believing to be believing *him*. For here again one can construct a funny sort of case – where you believe that what he believes will be true, but by accident, as it were. His belief is quite idiotic, he believes what he's got out of a Christmas cracker for example. In fact, unknown to him but known to you, what has been put in the crackers for their party are actual messages with some practical import. You know that the messages in the blue crackers are all true, and the ones in the red crackers all false. *He* believes any of them. And now he tells you something, and you believe it because he says it and you believe he is saying what he believes, *and* because you know that this thing that he believes comes out of a *blue* cracker. That wouldn't be believing *him*. But when you believe your history teacher, for example, it *is* enough that you believe what he says because he says it and you don't think he's lying and you think what he believes about that will be true. I mean, that is enough for you to be believing *him*.

So the topic of believing *someone* is pretty difficult. Of course if you could put in that you believe the person *knows* what he is telling you, these difficulties don't arise. You believe what he says because he says it and you believe that he knows whether it is so and won't be lying. That's why this par-

---

[1] I asked Mary Geach to construct a case to show this. She responded with what follows.

ticular problem won't normally arise about that letter from your friend Jones telling you his wife has just died.

Now there is another question about what it is to believe someone, which concerns the presuppositions. I said that *you* presuppose that Jones exists, did write the letter, and did say that in it, if you believe *him* to the effect that that was so. I didn't say that the mere fact of your *believing Jones* presupposed those things. Now what in fact are we to say here? Suppose someone has a hoax pen-friend – I mean, the pen-friend is really a contrivance of his school-fellows who arrange for their letters to be posted from Chicago to England and make the non-existent correspondent tell their friend all sorts of things. And suppose he believes the things in the usual sort of way in which people believe things they are told. Is he *believing the pen-friend?* What are we to say? Wouldn't we say that some ancient believed the oracles of the gods? And wouldn't it then be right to say he believed the god whose oracle it was?

If you insist on saying that the deluded victim does not 'believe the pen-friend' because the pen-friend doesn't exist, you will deprive yourself of the clearest way of describing his situation: "he believed this non-existent person". And, somewhat absurdly, you will have to say that his own expression of belief "I believe her", is *not* an expression of belief, or not a proper one. What then would be the proper one? We had better settle for saying that the victim believes the pen-friend, and that the ancient was believing Apollo – who does not exist. And doesn't the same point hold for the case where the letter-writer does exist, but you have misunderstood what he wrote, or mistakenly supposed that *this* letter is from him? Especially if the mistakes were quite reasonable ones.

Now let us think some more about the presuppositions. Ordinarily the presuppositions of believing N simply do not come in question. I get a letter from someone I know; it does not occur to me to doubt that it *is* from him. Suppose that the doubt *does* occur for some reason. The letter perhaps *says* it is from him – the very thing to raise a doubt! Now I take it as obvious that, if I decide to believe that the letter *is* from him, I won't do so on the grounds on which I believe *him* when the letter says his wife is dead. For I believe his wife is dead because *he* says so. But the reason why I believe the letter is from him is not that *he* says so. *His* credibility is not my warrant for believing that the letter is from him. Even if the letter begins "This is a letter from your old friend Jones" and I just believe that straight off and uncritically, I believe the sentence, and believe that the letter is from Jones because the sentence says so, but I could never say I believed it because I believed *him*. This is the sense in which the presuppositions of faith are not themselves part of the content of what in a narrow sense is believed by faith.

Now let us change the case. Suppose a prisoner in a dungeon, to whom there arrives a letter saying: 'This letter comes from an unknown friend, N.[2]

---

[2] This development of a case which I considered (see "What is it to believe someone?" in Volume II), of a letter from an otherwise unknown person, is taken from Peter Geach. See *The Virtues* (Cambridge, 1977).

It proposes to help him in various needs which he is invited to communicate by specified means. Perhaps it also holds out hope of escape from the prison. The prisoner doesn't know if it is a hoax or a trap or is genuine, but he tries the channels of communication and he gets some of the things that he asks for; he also gets further letters ostensibly from the same source. These letters sometimes contain information. We will suppose that he now believes that N exists and is the author of all the letters; and that he believes the information as coming from N. That is, his belief in that information is a case of believing N. His belief *that* N exists and that the letters come from N is, just as in the more ordinary case, not an example of believing something on N's say-so. On the other hand, as we are supposing the case, he does not have *prior* knowledge of N's existence. And it could happen that he, like the man who uncritically accepts the letter beginning "This is from Jones", believes the opening communication "This is from an unknown friend – call me N" straight off: just as he'd likely believe straight off that a whispered or tapped communication purporting to come from the next cell is a communication from another prisoner. Even so the beliefs which *are* cases of believing N and the belief *that* N exists are logically different. This brings out the difference between presuppositions of believing N and believing such-and-such as coming from N. "Pre-suppositions" don't have to be temporarily prior beliefs.

Suarez said that in every revelation God reveals that he reveals. That sounds like saying: every letter from N to the prisoner informs him that the information in the letter is from N, and every bit of information from N is accompanied by another bit of information that the first bit was from N. Put like that there is an absurdity, an infinite regress. But it should not be put like that. Rather: in every bit of information N is also claiming (implicitly or explicitly, it doesn't matter which) that he is giving the prisoner information.

And now we come to the difficulty. In all the other cases we have been considering, it can be made clear *what* it is for someone to believe someone. But what can it mean "to believe God"? Could a learned clever man inform me on the authority of his learning, that the evidence is that God has spoken? No. The only possible use of a learned clever man is as a *causa removens prohibens*. There are gross obstacles in the received opinion of my time and in its characteristic ways of thinking, and someone learned and clever may be able to dissolve these.

Forgetting that about 'hearing' – i.e. from teachers – should we picture it like this: a man hears a voice saying something to him and he believes it is God speaking, and so he believes what it says – so he believes God? But what does he believe when he 'believes it is God speaking'? That God has a voice-box? Hardly. In relation to the belief that it is God speaking, it doesn't matter how the voice is produced. There is a Rabbinical idea, the Bath Qol, the 'daughter of the voice'. You hear a sentence as you stand in a crowd – a few words out of what someone is saying perhaps: it leaps out at you, it 'speaks to your condition'. Thus there was a man standing in a crowd and he heard a woman saying "Why are you wasting your time?" He had been dithering about, putting off the question of becoming a Catholic. The voice struck him to the heart and he acted in obedience to it. Now, he did not have to suppose, nor did he suppose, that that remark was not made in the course of some exchange between the woman and her companion, which had nothing to do with him. But he believed that God had spoken to him in that voice. The same thing happened to St Augustine, hearing the child's cry, "Tolle, lege".

Now the criticial differentiating point is this. In all those other cases it is clear what the one who 'believes X' *means* by "X speaking", even when we judge that X doesn't exist. For example, what the believer in the oracle means by "Apollo speaking". But it is not clear what it can mean for God to speak.

For Apollo, or Juggernaut, is simply the god of such and such a cult. Note, I am not here following those who explain deity as "the object of worship". That definition is useless, because they have to mean by "worship" "the honour paid to a *deity*". Divine worship is the special sort of honour intended to be paid, the special sort of address made, to a deity. This may be offered to what is not divine, to a stone or another spirit or a man; or to what doesn't exist at all.

So when I say "Apollo was the god of such-and-such a cult", I am calling attention to the question: what would it mean to say "These were not – none of them were – the temples and oracles of Apollo" – precisely *of* the temples and oracles of Apollo? What would it mean to say that Shiva was not the god of destruction? Shiva is the god of this worship, which is the cultus of a god of destruction.

In this sense, God is not the god of such-and-such a worship. This is something that can be seen by an atheist too, even though he holds that there is in any case no such thing as deity. For he can see, if he thinks about it, that "God" is not a proper name but is equivalent to a 'definite description' (in the technical sense). That is, it is equivalent to "the one and only true god", "the one and only real deity". The point of putting in "true" and "real" is that those who believe there is only one deity have so much occasion to speak of deities that they do not believe to exist. We then speak of Apollo, Shiva and Juggernaut as gods who are not gods. An atheist believes that God is among the gods who are not gods, because he believes that nothing is a deity. But he should be able to recognize the identity of "God" with "the one and only god".

It is because of this equivalence that God cannot be formally identified as the god of such-and-such a cult or such-and-such a people. To say that God is the god of Israel is to say that what Israel worshipped as god was 'the one and only god'. So it *could* significantly be denied. And it *could* be seen to be true – even by one who believed that the description 'the one and only god' is vacuous.

And so we can say this: the supposition that someone has faith is the supposition that he believes that something – it may be a voice, it may be something he has been taught – comes as a word from God. Faith is then the belief he accords that word.

So much can be discerned by an unbeliever, whether his attitude is potentially one of reverence in face of this phenomenon or is only hostile. But the Christian adds that such a belief is sometimes the truth, and that the consequent belief is only then what *he* means by faith.

Part Three

Political Philosophy

13 On Frustration of the Majority by Fulfilment of the Majority's Will

Where matters are decided, yes or no, by a majority vote, the decision on each matter is the will of the majority. But it is also possible that the majority should vote in the minority on a majority of the questions. This may be shown in a table.

	A	B	C	D	E	F	G	H	I	J	K
1	0	1	1	1	1	0	0	1	1	0	0
2	0	1	0	1	1	0	0	1	0	1	1
3	0	1	0	0	1	0	0	1	1	1	1
4	0	1	0	0	0	1	1	0	1	1	1
5	0	0	0	0	1	1	1	0	1	1	1
6	0	0	0	0	0	1	1	1	1	1	1
7	0	0	0	0	0	1	1	1	1	1	1
8	1	0	0	0	0	0	1	1	1	1	1
9	1	0	1	0	0	0	0	1	1	1	1
10	1	0	1	1	0	0	0	1	1	0	1
11	1	0	1	1	0	0	0	1	0	1	1

Here we have eleven voters, A–K, voting on eleven questions. Seven of them, A–G, vote in the minority in a majority of the decisions: A–F in seven out of the eleven cases, G in six. The majority is always 6–5. These figures can of course be varied.

If we imagine an ideal democracy with a whole population voting directly on all questions, there will obviously be room for much variation in results over a long period, all of which, however, conform to the description: the majority votes in the minority in a majority of cases.

This fact, I thought when I stumbled on it, must be familiar to voting experts. But I have not found it remarked upon. It sometimes startles people, eliciting the reaction: "But doesn't this make nonsense of democracy?"

In the West, and perhaps in the whole world where Western forms of education prevail, men are brought up in a conviction of the unique fairness of democracy. It is even conceived to be as it were the sole legitimate form of government. "It's not democratic" is a condemnation. Pope Pius XII once spoke in a Christmas allocution of the right of democracies to defend themselves by whatever means they might think necessary. One could hardly have better proof of the pervasiveness of the attitude, if of all people the Pope of Rome should speak as if democracies had some special entitlement.

From *Analysis*, 36, 4 (1976).

Outside governments, we notice that methods of proceeding and alterations in arrangements are often proposed on no other ground than that they will be 'more democratic'. I know a university, for example, where on these grounds representation in the authoritative assembly was made proportional to the numbers in the different departments. Large departments proceeded to forbid expansion to or even to reduce small ones, increasing themselves as every opportunity offered.

In the liberal tradition of the West, democracy has certainly been favoured, and belief in it instilled as a fundamental dogma. But there are other strands belonging to that tradition. One of them is a concern for minorities. Upholders of this, it seems, were conscious that a majority may be a cruel and oppressive bully to a minority. In consequence 'protection of minorities' or 'of the rights of minorities' also had a certain sacred flavour. This it perhaps sometimes retains more in the United States than in England, where a common denigratory phrase nowadays is "merely sectional interests". However this may be, I notice in my own country at least a hardening of sentiment exclusively in favour of democracy, which is sometimes also called "majority rule". Such is the sentiment in favour of this, that it is not *astonishing* to hear of an apparently reasonable and well-disposed man who says: someone who is not prepared to accept a majority decision, or a law enacted by democratic processes, ought to leave the society. And this, without any limitation's being put on what the matter of the law or decision may be. We see that from such a mind the liberal tradition of concern for the 'rights of minorities' has been nearly expunged.

Let us consider the *rationale* of the idea that decision according to the will of the majority is superior to any other. That a particular decision according to the will of a majority may be inferior, in the sense of stupider, is evident. I take it that a decision is stupid if its implementation is undesirable from the point of view of the very people who wanted it. They would have it: but when they get it, it is evident that they would rather not have it; if they had only realized what it would be like for their decision to be implemented, it would not have been made. There was another decision available, perhaps: if the power of making the decision had not been taken away from some particular person and vested in the majority. And it is now recognized that *that* decision would have been better.

The superiority of the majority decision cannot reside in its necessarily superior wisdom. A superiority, even when the decision is stupid, is rather thought to be in this: participation in the decision-making is itself valuable; or perhaps one should say, is itself *a value*. Such a value is mystical of course. I don't mean a criticism in saying so. But consider a man who always or most often finds himself voting in the minority, and who judges that most of the decisions taken are extremely harmful. Why may he nevertheless extol this method of arriving at decisions? He may think that alternatives available in the situation would lead to even worse ones, but that is not to put a value on participation as such. He may feel some satisfaction with the method in that there *was* always a contrary voice, and that his made part of it – but why? Honour satisfied? That *is* mystical. A nucleus of possible opposition and difference of direction? There may be none such: the minorities in which he votes may be inconstant sets of people. Does he simply have a 'we' feeling about the decisions, bad as he thinks they are? "*We* decide for ourselves" – even though *his* vote was always contrary to the decision? There is indeed such a sentiment, but, once again, it is mystical. He has reason to feel as oppressed by the authority of the majority as he might by the authority of an autocrat or superior body, who 'hands down' decisions that he has to accept.

Now there is a quite different belief to yield the superiority of majority decision except, indeed, where it is stupid in the sense I have explained. Let us suppose a set of people who have to determine, or for whom it must be determined, what they shall do or what shall happen to them collectively. Suppose that they are all going to go somewhere in a vehicle; the question is, where? Some would like to go to one place, some to another. They can't go to both. But they must all go together where they go. Doesn't it then seem reasonable that they should go where the majority of them want to go? All cannot be satisfied; in this way, perhaps, most of them will be. Complications arise, of course, where the choices are multiple; but let me assume just a simple choice, made by everyone, between a pair of alternatives. Then the majority, if there is one, will be absolute. Now it does seem most reasonable that, where all cannot have their way, the greater number should not be frustrated.

Note that *this* defence of majority decision in conveniently simple cases does not assume that there is actually a value in people's sharing the job of making the decision. For the argument only concerns people's getting what they want.

The reasonableness is meant to consist in a sort of fairness. If the desires of the majority are not to prevail, then a few perhaps get what they want at the expense of a greater number who do not. This seems to put the desires of those few in a privileged position; which is intrinsically unfair. When the majority get what they want, they do so at the expense of the minority's frustration, but at least nobody is privileged; for the upshot results from making the desire of each count equally. *Ex hypothesi* no upshot could satisfy all equally; a method which derives the upshot from an equal weight attached to each person's desire must achieve the satisfaction of the desires of the greatest possible number and so be both the best and fairest.

This belief about the best and fairest upshot is independent of the method adopted to secure that upshot. If the method adopted can be that of majority vote on simple alternatives this, it is arguable, is the best method because presumably people are themselves in the best position to know what they want. Even though they may sometimes make mistakes, that is worth putting up with, because they will surely, at least for the most part, vote for what they really do want. But the method of majority decision is here espoused, not because of any intrinsic value in people's sharing in making decisions, but on the assumption that it is the best available method for securing the upshot. The argument that this is the best and fairest upshot does not depend on this being the method for securing it; but, stupidity apart, this method would secure it more surely than any other.

Note that that way of looking at the merits of majority decision starts off with an assumption: namely, that a decision has to be made for people *as a collection*; a decision has to be made which determines what everyone does or has in some matter. This was why I supposed the case where it was given that a party of people were in for going somewhere in a vehicle. We should distinguish between this set of people and a set of people in a house who happen to have a practice of determining daily by majority decision what all of them are going to do that day. Here one might say: "Why not let each choose his own activity?" and the argument I gave purporting to show that the will of the majority should prevail will have no force.

At least, it will have no force until we take into account that some people's desired activities include making other people act in various ways. The philosopher that I referred to, who thought that one had no right to remain in a society if one was not prepared to accept its majority decisions, did not stipulate that the decisions should concern only actions and fates where a decision for a whole collection of people is necessary. This is perhaps realistic for the following reason: some people desire to control others, to dictate to them, as also to get them (in various ways) to do things they would not otherwise do. Now if our initial assumption is: each person's desire shall have as much weight as anyone else's in calculating what to do – then these types of desire can't be excluded from consideration. As soon as there is a proposal to interfere with X's activity, someone presumably wants to do so. If interfering can come up for majority decision at all, and it is proposed, some want and some perhaps do not want a decision that that set of people collectively interfere with X. Even if those prevail who do not want to interfere with X and do not want it to be a collective decision to interfere with X, it has come about that there necessarily is a collective decision *whether* to interfere with X.[1] What reason could be offered against the paramountcy of the will of the majority? The 'given', that they are 'in for' some decision (as it was a 'given' that my set of people were going somewhere in their vehicle), has been contrived merely by the question's coming up for majority decision at all.

Contrast the situation of an autocrat; he is the source of all the decisions about collections of people. He is also so powerful that he can interfere with any arbitrary X if he likes. If he does so (or abstains) his action remains an action just relating to X; it is not transformed into a decision about people collectively.

I do not want to steer further out into these deep waters. For my quarry is something quite different. We had an argument purporting to show that,

---

[1] May there not be some liberties which only stand so long as they are not brought into consideration? Bringing them into consideration is *already* making them subject to decision.

where there are a lot of people collectively in for one of a pair of alternatives, the best and fairest decision was the alternative preferred by the majority. It seemed *best* because we are envisaging no criterion of what is good except that it is wanted, or of evil except frustration of desire; it seemed *fairest* because everyone's desire is given equal weight. The tradition of concern for minorities is nourished by far different considerations than these. What those may be is not at all my concern. I am impressed by the argument, even if I would like to draw from some other source some principle of limitation of its applicability.

But now – the table presented right at the beginning seems to damage this argument, which at first seems so impressive. For what do we have here? Each decision is made according to a majority vote. Each decision, then (folly apart), would seem to be the best and fairest. But when we look back and forth through many decisions, a different picture emerges. No need to worry about minorities yet! The majority is frustrated more often than not! Doesn't this destroy the original argument? For what was appealing about the satisfaction of the preference of the majority was precisely this: granted that all cannot be satisfied, the best is that most should be; the principle of letting the desire of each have equal weight will both secure this and in itself be fair, because none is given privileged consideration in the decisions as they come up.

But the table shows that the best and the fairest (by that criterion) may part company when we look through a multitude of decisions. However paradoxical it may be, it seems that the principle of the majority getting what they want allows the majority to get what they do *not* want in a majority of cases. The air of paradox is only partly produced by its looking as if some set of people, called 'the majority', were the same in both parts of the observation – as of course, it is not. That it is not only shows that what seemed paradoxical is not viciously so at all. It does not show that there is any error in the judgement: "So in this way the majority may be frustrated!"

Note that this is not a point just about the method of decision by majority vote. I have been at pains to distinguish that from the principle of the decision's being what the majority wants. The method of majority decision may be regarded as *a* method for securing the latter. But the paradox to which I have pointed applies to the principle itself as well as to the method of majority decision.

It will now be plain why I have assumed the simplest possible kind of issues as the matter of decision, and assumed a perfect democracy in which all concerned vote quite directly. It is a familiar point that different voting procedures, multiple choices, what is motion and what is amendment, and other such matters, make such a difference to results that the will of the majority can seem to be uncapturable, or even non-existent. Also, we don't have pure, but rather delegated, democracies. One is inclined to say: "If only everything were simple, the total population concerned voting on straight Yes–No alternatives without any question of rigging (by nature or design) from the order in which they were taken – if only things were like that, *then* we'd have the ideal satisfied (to the extent that people weren't stupid) of the greatest possible number of people getting what they want." What the table shows is that this is an illusion. We ought therefore to give up any idea of achieving as good an approximation as possible to that ideally simple kind of result, which can itself be achieved only in very simple situations. Where the ideal is actually achieved the achievement of the further ideal is by no means guaranteed.

It may be, indeed, that the criterion of fairness appeals to us: the criterion by which the desire of each has equal weight in each decision. But when we look back and forth through many decisions, a different idea of fairness in satisfaction obtrudes itself. Thus a parent of a large family might say: "Each child shall *take its turn* to decide such-and-such – *that* will be fair."

Someone may say: "The possibility which you have pointed to does not matter at all, even if it is often actualized. (And, by the way, you don't know whether it is often, never, or very seldom actualized.)[2] It is simply evident that majority decision is a sound way for a group of reasonable, equal, autonomous beings to determine what is best to do. That being so, it is of no import if, over many decisions, the method leads to this result. What matters is the determination of *each* question in the best way."

To see both the force and the weakness of this comment, let us imagine a method of majority judgement instead of majority decision. Our case will be rather artificial, but no matter. We will suppose some matter of fleeting observation of which constant record is needed, and where the observation always decides between a pair of alternatives. The matter being difficult, a team of observers is always employed, and what is put down in the record each time is the observation of the majority. This gives rise to just the same possibility as we have been discussing for decisions. When you look through a series of such results, you may find that the majority of the team have made the minority observation in a majority of the cases. But there would be nothing disturbing about this. If the method for determining what is to go in the record deserves criticism, that will not be because of *this* possibility; if the possibility is actualized, that is just a 'giddy parergon', a merely incidental curiosity. It has no tendency to invalidate a 'principle of majority observation'. For all that matters is the determination of each result at the time. The same might hold if the principle of majority judgement were used in trials with a constant panel of judges.[3]

Such no doubt is the thought of our objector. He is saying: "All that matters is the determination of each cause at the time in the best way." But that can hardly be right, except on the assumption that there is an objectively best or good decision to make, the best way of determining which is to take a majority vote. By "an objectively best or good decision" I mean a decision

---

[2] It would be of some interest, perhaps, to scrutinize the voting in the English Parliament of the early eighteenth century with just this question in mind.

[3] My colleague J. E. J. Altham has remarked to me that the smallest number for which this result is obtainable is five.

which is best or good independently of what people want. Well, if anyone can give such an account, more power to him! But as we have been considering the matter, all that is in question *is* what, given their circumstances, people actually want, which in the individual case a man gets by his choice or action if it is not stupid.[4] But in the case where people must do or suffer something collectively, the idea was that the majority should get what they want. So the frustration of the majority when we consider a whole series of majority decisions – the failure of the majority to have got what they want more often than not – cannot be regarded just as a mildly curious by-product.

Indeed, we might see in our problem a way of giving a real meaning to the rhetorically attractive but actually senseless expression "the greatest happiness of the greatest number". This is of the same form as "the greatest number of words in the shortest time".[5] and when we have two things actually countable and measurable like words and times we see that it makes no sense. But we might say that what the famous phrase intends *can* be given a sense: at least it can if "minimal frustration of the majority" has one. How this could be planned for is indeed difficult to see. It might have to involve departing from the method of majority decision by the population.

That, of course, we do depart from anyway; we have delegated democracy, and use majority decision in committees and Parliaments. The aim of their decisions is not supposed to be satisfying the desires of the majority of their own membership. *Here*, then, the objection that I considered has a point; there is not necessarily anything to worry about, if the majority of a committee should turn out to have voted in the minority in the majority of issues it has decided.

Let us turn, then, to the question of satisfying the majority desire, on any given issue, of the whole of a community or population. As remarked, my table need not be a voting table: it may represent a set of questions being decided (no matter how) in accordance with, or contrary to, the will of people (or groups) A–K. Here then we see the naked point: the majority may be satisfied on every issue, while nevertheless the majority is frustrated over a majority of issues. There is thus the possibility of a certain technique of tyranny whose every measure has the support and is truly in accord with the desire of the majority, those whom any given measure hurts being in the minority; or again, one by one 'merely sectional interests' are damaged. Since everyone not wretchedly isolated belongs to several 'sections', it will be possible for the tyrant to damage the interests of anyone or any group (that does not support him, say) while truthfully claiming 'democratic' support for his measures. Or again, the process of damage to sectional interests – that is, to a majority of the population – may occur in a democracy in a haphazard fashion and without design, always in accordance with the will of the majority.

[4] This is not in fact true, because "the race is not to the swift etc." But the falsity of it cannot play a part in our considerations.

[5] The comparison was passed on to me by Gareth Evans, but I think he said he did not invent it.

14   On the Source of the Authority of the State

I

My question is: how the state, or again how government, can be justified.

The question may seem a silly one because, like it or not, we are stuck with the state. But it is after all not silly, because we can take up different attitudes to being governed. As Aristotle said about philosophy: if there isn't an enquiry to make, there *is* an enquiry. The conclusion that the pretensions of civil authority lack justification tells us not to look for a foundation, the thing is merely there. But that conclusion, if it is justified, is justified only by such an enquiry. A Marxist believes in the 'withering away of the state' after the dictatorship of the proletariat has exercised the powers of government in the last phase of the class war. He, therefore, has not got to tell us the theory of the state when its institutions, laws, courts, armies, police, prisons, systems of property, etc., are something other than weapons in the class war: for it will no longer be there. That should mean, not that he thinks he can show that there isn't a question, but that he has already decided that the state with its institutions is evil. If it is, then our attitude to it may be purely pragmatic, or may be determined by a revolutionary goal. But the question itself has not been rejected: however implicitly, it has been answered.

Whether one's attitude to 'legitimate government' should be always, ever, or just sometimes that of acknowledgement of authority is a potentially serious question for everyone. I suppose that will readily be granted. But to many, especially philosophers, at the present day, it will appear as a 'moral' question. Legal authority, legal validity, legal obligation: these are one thing; their presence or absence is to be ascertained by looking at certain institutions and their rules. It is another question altogether whether one should grant moral authority, moral validity and moral obligation. Assuming no quarrel about whether the government is what is called 'legitimate', that is essentially a personal and private question. Now I suppose I understand as well as anyone the point of someone's saying: "This is what I am legally obliged to do, but it would be, e.g., an act of horrid injustice, and so I refuse to go along with my legal obligation." But I am struck by the following: one might say the exactly corresponding thing about an obligation arising under the rules of some club that one belonged to. The difference between the two is that one can resign from the club and so escape the obligation arising under its rules, but one can't very well resign from being governed. This raises the question: suppose the club (something like the Jacobin Club) grew tremendously powerful, became able to control anything it wanted to in the society, to extort money and sequester property from whom it chose; to issue and enforce edicts affecting people at large, and suppose it forbade resignation of its members; what then would be the difference between the judgement: "This is what I am obliged to do by the rules of the club . . ." and that other judgement 'This is what I am legally obliged to do . . .'? I am not necessarily supposing that the two are made together in the same place, though I suppose they might be. Cf. what one hears about the Mafia and the government in southern Italy. If we want to understand civil authority, we need to distinguish there being a government exercising civil authority from two contrasting things: on the one side, from large-scale voluntary co-operative associations, and on the other from a place's being quite under the control of a smooth sophisticated Mafia. It seems clear that this is not a private or personal question, not a question to be answered by consulting one's 'moral intuitions' or debating inwardly whether one thinks oneself 'morally' obliged to obey the exercisers of power.

Starting with the former, we shall see what distinguishes civil authority from the authority to be found in voluntary associations. For here too we find authority. It comes in two kinds. When courses of action are adopted, ends and means taken towards them aren't the only things looked to or implicitly invoked in determining what is done. Someone or some group (up to the whole membership) must make decisions. "Authority" may stand for a personal characteristic: what a certain person says or presses for is felt as weighty. This is the first kind. But authority is also vested in the various rules or customs used in determining matters; there is, say, a definite procedure for deciding, and appeal is made to rule or custom in doing so. Both these sorts of authority I call "weight relative to free decisions". People are allowed to pull out. There is then not an unconditional demand for obedience (except the demand that one either comply or get out of the committee or the association, etc.). Authority here, then, is quite different from that of the state.

Not that such a demand is the peculiar mark of a state. Obviously it is made by parents, teachers, gangsters, slave-owners, employers of indentured labour, religious superiors. A further distinguishing mark of the authority of the state is the exercise, actual or threatened, of institutional violent coercive power. I say "institutional" to exclude its being personal, casual or sporadic. Calling it institutional signifies that it is a norm of a continuing organization for there to be this threat. And, in particular, that there are some people effectually ordered by others to make the threat and sometimes to exert the violence. But again, I don't use the word "norm" as it were to canonize or sanctify, to suggest validity of some sort. For I would call it institutional violent coercive power if a town were taken over and run in a systematic fashion by a bandit gang. Here would be organization in which there were different roles, and violence or the threat of it would be a norm. It would thus be institutional. The gang, we suppose, is supreme in power.

But we shouldn't have civil authority as that is generally understood.

One might say, shortly: government is distinguished from authority in voluntary co-operative enterprises by 'bearing the sword', by its exercise, actual and threatened, of coercive force. And: *if* it is distinguished from the control of a place by a gang of bandits, it is so by its authority in the command of violence. This portmanteau phrase covers (1) authority to lay commands and prohibitions on people, which are backed up by the threat of coercion, and to lay down forms for doing and determining things in such a way that decisions can be enforced and (2) authority to order some people to use force on others.

Authority on the part of those who give orders and make regulations is: a right to be obeyed. More amply, we may say: authority is a regular right to be obeyed in a domain of decision.

It might be thought that the difference we are seeking could be stated, not as one of authority, but as one of the domain of concern. But that is not so. We may suppose that our gangsters want things orderly. And beyond that very superficial indication, how can we specify a domain of concern which is special to government, and of no interest to gangsters? It is indeed one of the troubles about government, that it is difficult to specify the 'things that are Caesar's'. If a government concerns itself with no matter what, then even to comment on the subject of its concern is to enter the domain of 'politics'.

The picture of the problem that I am drawing may seem to be fantastic. Here in England, for example, a minister of the Crown cannot single me out and tell me what to do and what not, just because he would like to, using the police to back him up if I am recalcitrant. I and many others feel pretty safe from 'arbitrary' demands. That is surely very different from what we imagine of gangsters running a place. They can decide 'arbitrarily' that some individual must do or suffer what suits *them*.

But now, just what distinction have we in mind here? That the gangster decisions relate to an individual directly, rather than because he is a member of some class? This would suggest that in Acts of Attainder the English Parliament adopted the posture of gangsters. Perhaps they did. But it would be a bold legal theorist who would say that legislation, let alone governmental decision, could never refer directly to individuals.

Or is it the lack of procedure? Well, must a government, to be a government, always be non-arbitrary in its actions? And, may not a gang of bandits be all tied up with rules of procedure? Remember my imaginary jumped-up club. Our gangsters may be a large efficient organization, so institutional in character that men outside the organization are in general ordered to do this, prohibited from doing that, made the victims of extortion (of money and other things too), threatened with violence if they disobey, merely as each one falls under some general classification, and there may be formalities. May not the agents of our gang act much like 'officials'?

"But you can't imagine gangsters being so self-restrictive! Even if the common run of people are under their heel only as each falls into some classification, even if there are rules of procedure and a smooth organization, the gangsters will be a lawless lot at the top. Succession to positions of power will often be by acts of murder, for example." But the like has also often been heard of among what are counted as governments.

"But government is for the benefit of the governed, banditry for the profit of the bandits! Of course, a regime may not succeed in benefiting its people, it may do rather a lot of harm. But the general idea of government is the idea of something good for and necessary to 'men in multitudes'. The idea of banditry is of something whose point is to rob people. A bandit who enriches himself by the opportunities of his profession is doing the work and attaining the end of a bandit: a ruler or politician who does the same does it, we must earnestly say, only *per accidens*." This Aristotelian mode of thought helps us to see the distinction. But now is it because of *that* distinction that ordinary people under government can feel safe, unimpeded and unthreatened? Surely not! Not everyone feels safe under government; some may feel safe under a robber chief.

Suppose it were suggested that we were merely conditioned not to want to go through locked doors. It is an illusion that I am unimpeded. I submit to the impediments. I let the knowledge of the restrictions and the dangers I would incur in taking certain courses modify my will to act. I have much free play, like a joint in a socket: it is seldom that some definite thing is absolutely required of me, like paying a tax bill. If I lived in a place that was rather smoothly run by the Mafia, would I not then too let the conditions modify my will to act? Then I, together with many others, might feel as safe and unimpeded and unthreatened as people do under many governments.

So does the difference lie in the good purposes of government? The comparison with bandits was suggested just by the use and threat of physical coercion which mark the state. If good purposes are the distinction, then we shall want an answer to the following question: if some people want to do good, does that give them the right to threaten me and make rules about my behaviour? Or: does it give them such a right, if there is already a long established practice of the same kind, already a body of rules made by predecessors of theirs, an established organization within which they go about their work?

If so, it will no doubt be some improvement in the situation for me if they themselves proceed by rules and go through formalities. I shall know better what to expect. An Italian painter of the Renaissance did a 'Decollation of St John' for the Great Turk. The Sultan, looking at the picture, remarked that the painter did not know the anatomy of the neck, and at a flick of his fingers the head of a bystanding slave rolled on the floor for the instruction of the painter. That shows what one means by "arbitrary"! By contrast, the proceeding would not be 'arbitrary' if there were an already existing ministerial regulation or Parliamentary enactment providing for the instruction of visiting painters, and someone had to sign a formal order. But if there have to be victims, the non-arbitrariness seems not to be much mitigation of their wrongs. Indeed, neither the non-arbitrariness nor the beneficent intention seems to serve. Lest I seem to be speaking too exotically, recall that there are current movements of thought in the direction of a requirement to make some people's organs available for transplant into others.

Our brief statement, then, is vindicated, and the question that arises is: with what right may people, in various ways exercising the power of the state, lay violence and threats of violence on anyone? For the distinction between the Mafia and a government is first and foremost that a government has authority in its doings. I do not say that the doings can be all just the same, the government having authority to do these things and the Mafia not. But *some* of the doings of government and its officers are distinguished from very similar doings of gangsters by that fact, and that is crucial.

We ask what can be the source of such a right, if it exists. And at the present level of enquiry, the answer cannot be law, because – to put it crudely – we are asking for the source of a right to lay laws on people at all.

The notion of 'a right' is one that we have some idea how to operate with, but it is unsatisfactory not to have an account of it. Indeed, a clear derivation of the right we are considering won't be possible without some account. I will give one a little later. But first, I will sketch my account of the source.

There are three sources to consider: (I will not spend time here arguing this.) They are: prescription, contract and task.

In traditional language a 'prescriptive' right is a customary right, a right established purely by custom: "prescription" in this connection is another word for custom. It is clear that to the extent that we can speak of property among men in a state of nature, i.e. without legal institutions, property rights are prescriptive. *If* a slave owner could ever be said to have a right to the obedience of his slaves, this must have been basically a prescriptive right, however fortified it may have been by laws. (The 'right of conquest' was a prescriptive right.[1]) If you say to a guest in your house: "Please do not go into my study," this has the force of a prohibition even though the form of a polite request, and your authority in the matter is prescriptive.

I will not immediately debate the rationale of, or the *a priori* limits on, the possibility of prescriptive authority, though I will later offer a calculation by which the authority of government cannot be merely that. Here I mention prescriptive rights only to set them on one side, wanting to say something fairly general about the ground of authority. Namely, that the ground of authority is most often a task. Authority arises from the necessity of a task whose performance requires a certain sort and extent of obedience on the part of those for whom the task is supposed to be done. If I said that this was always the sole ground of authority, I should be wrong; for there is such a thing as prescriptive authority (as the case of the guest makes clear). There is also contractually conceded authority. But this must be voluntary, and it terminates when the contract does. The interesting cases of authority are

---

[1] We should distinguish between regular slavery and the condition of the Athenian prisoners in the quarry at Syracuse, or the prisoners regularly worked to death in the Krupps and I.G. Farben factories under the Nazis.

those where *the subjects of authority are so willy-nilly*. Apart from prescriptions, these are always cases where the authority, if there *is* authority, stems from the task. Parental authority, for example, and – as I shall argue – governmental authority. You find yourself the subject of these whether you like it or not. Parental authority diminishes and finally lapses as the task is accomplished – or the time for doing it is over. But government is always with us. In the present state of the planet one can hardly escape beyond the frontiers of government. (It is interesting that in the last century, when it still looked as if people could do just that, a legal maxim was invoked or invented: *Nemo potest exuere patriam* – no one can shuck off his country – to deny this. The Boers, pressing into hitherto ungoverned regions, were held merely to extend the domain of the government that claimed to rule them where they were before.)

Authority stemming from a task does not indeed relate only to obedience. I mean that obedience and disobedience are not the only correlative responses to it. We see this where we speak of parental authority in relations other than the obedience of their children. A small baby does not obey, but we may acknowledge the authority of a parent in decisions about what should be done with it. So authority might be thought to be a right to decide in some domain, and its correlate not to be obedience, but respect. For you can go against someone's authority not merely by being a disobedient subject of it, but also by being an interfering outsider. Nevertheless this is secondary. We would not speak of someone's authority in every case where we admit his right to decide – e.g. in matters of his own dress. Here "authority" would be a redundant notion. So obedience/disobedience are the (logically) primary correlates of authority, i.e. the correlates without which there would be no such distinctive thing as authority (in our present sense); and, following upon this, there are *also* the correlative responses of respect, non-impediment and their opposites.

Not that we can define authority by its having obedience/disobedience as its correlative responses. For gangsters can command obedience. If we are to make the distinction we want, we have to speak of a right to obedience.

Since a distinctive thing about civil government, as opposed to people's having dominant positions in common enterprises, is actual or threatened violence, it is either an evil or a necessity based on evil. If we were not dangerous to one another, if humans could be trusted not to violate one another's persons and unjustly impede one another's activities, there could be no need of government involving coercive power.

It is possible to hold that the human world is one in which some of the bandits have got on top, so that their claim to a right in exercising power is just a huge trick. Thus Alexander the Great once caught a pirate, and asked him to explain himself. The man replied, "I do in a small way what you do in a big way." This may be called the pure pacifist position. Alexander was somewhat taken by the man and made him a provincial governor, a task which I believe he executed competently.

Or it is possible to hold that because it will be that some men do not leave others in peace, though these are peaceable, but will attack them and violently impede their activities and enterprises, it is after all a human need that there should be government and laws backed by force: people legally making decisions which can impose on all those on whom they impinge, and standing forces providing the backing.

If someone holds in a sufficiently radical fashion that government is a refined and grandiose banditry, it is hardly possible to convince him of error. It is, he says, a system whereby some people, who are able and willing to command violence, have succeeded in getting on top, and these clothe themselves in the luxurious cloak of 'authority'. He is as it were blind to everything but the evil of violence, which he is unable to concede may ever be just. This is an axiom for him.

Anyone who does think this ought to be clear about it. He ought not to be selective. If he is willing to invoke the law, to take anyone to court, or to call on the police for protection, then he should regard himself as making use of some available members of a bandit gang.

That is to say, one shouldn't deceive oneself by failing to recognize that the civil power essentially 'bears the sword': that what we have here is canonized violence.

True, the more successful and better used civil authority is, the less will this be apparent; the less actual use of violence on the part of the civil authority there will be. But the threat of it, the readiness to be violent to the point of killing where there are violent law-breakers – that is always there. No political theory can be worth a jot, that does not acknowledge the violence of the state, or face the problem of distinguishing between states and syndicates. There is a famous saying of St Augustine's: "*Remota justitia, quid sunt regna nisi magna latrocinia?*" This was difficult to translate, but modern institutions have given us the word: "Take away justice, and what are States but big Syndicates?" Now this might suggest that you 'only' need to add justice to force – i.e. to postulate that what is enjoined or aimed at by those exercising the force is what would otherwise be just – to render the state just. But there is the question what renders it just to exercise force in, say, requiring what is just. The parent may in effect say "Don't hit your little brother, or I will hit you." What is the difference – *is* there a difference – between his threat and the threat of the child he so threatens? After all, the little brother may have been doing something quite unfair. The same question arises about the violence of the state. I judge that this is the fundamental question of political theory.

It may be objected to this thesis and to resultant theses *that civil power is either an evil or is based on evil*: "You have missed the real nub of the matter. It is true that human beings are malignantly dangerous to one another. But that (for so long as it remains so) merely gives the state one of its tasks. And if it were not so, government would still be needed. It is no evil, in the sense either of malice or of defect, that individuals cannot severally and separately calculate what enterprises to give prior place, what activities to limit for the sake of other ones. Co-operative enterprises and procedures are needed for the enhancement of life – without them it would be poor and often short, even though it were not entirely solitary nasty and brutish. But, where you have 'men in multitudes', such enterprises will sometimes collide. A machinery of decision will be needed, which is above the special enterprises, and which perhaps initiates some of them too. And besides that there are many proceedings, such as getting married, forming various sorts of association, disposing of property, for which either custom or explicit rule must provide the forms, so that people can 'know where they are'. Only in very simple societies is custom sufficient. Here again we need a machinery for fixing the forms and determining what has been in accord with them; and it needs to be connected with the machinery for decision between colliding enterprises. 'Utopianly' this machinery, acknowledged by all (for we are supposing humans without vice, hence without that of stupidity) and never working contrary to wisdom and justice, nor needing any violence to support it, would be something like a government. It would indeed *be* government in the ideal situation. It is wrong to concentrate on an unfortunate incidental task which arises from man's disordered state, and say that *that* gives us the essential mark of civil authority."

To this I reply: no, it is not wrong. For I raised the question: what distinguishes the state from a voluntary association? and the present objection says no more than: "If there were no malignancy among humans, there would be voluntary association in having something like government – a topmost authority fixing forms and adjudicating between colliding enterprises." That is to say that, were there no human malignity, my problem of finding that distinction would not arise. At most there would be a question of distinguishing civil society from other forms of voluntary association. I said that the interesting cases of authority are those where the subjects of authority are so willy-nilly. In the 'Utopian' conception, there is no 'nilly'. My imaginary opponent spoke of the unfortunate incidental task which arose from man's disordered state. But of two things one: either my thesis has already been conceded, or the need for the machinery of decision spoken of does not yet show us anything about a government's right to coerce resistant wills.

Here is the point at which we need to enquire: what is a right? We need to do so, that is, unless we are willing without more ado to accept the following as a valid *form* of argument: men in multitudes need governments, need laws backed by force and people exercising the powers of government. Therefore it is possible that there should be people exercising these powers as of right. But the performance of the task of government is not possible unless there is extensive civic obedience, and unless there is also force at the command of those exercising its powers, which force they have a right to command. Therefore those who by right exercise the powers of government have authority in the sense which I have argued we need.

The next section, in which I explain what a right is at all, is addressed to the further needs of philosophy, especially at the present day, and to all besides who are beset by the feeling that 'this is a moral question, and morality is purely relative and cultural, or a matter of a person's prejudices'. Anyone without these needs can skip the next section and proceed to the third one. There I argue for the premises of the above argument and maintain that the authority of the state cannot rise by a transfer of individual rights, and that there is a certain intrinsic limit to it.

II

The notion of a right is very fundamental and philososophically very intractable. It seems absurd to introduce it as an unexplained primitive. But how to explain it? No one has succeeded in this. At best, thinkers have sorted out distinctions within and around the notion, have noted some of its logical features, and so on. They have noted, for example, that a right is a right of someone against someone else. My right not to be molested cannot be infringed by a lion that mauls me or a boulder that falls on me. Only persons can infringe rights, only persons can have them. We may also note the variations in rights in respect of waivability, transferability, etc., and the opposites of these. Justice as a personal virtue is that character in a man which means that he has a settled determination not to infringe anyone's right. A wrong is an infringement of a right. What is wrong about an act that is wrong may be just this, that it is *a* wrong. All this we may understand, and we may wish also to say much about actual rights, but we are still nowhere near explaining the concept of a right.

A right is not a natural phenomenon that can be discerned and named as a feature found in some class of creatures by, say, a taxonomist. It is in this respect like a rule and a promise: that 'natural unintelligibility' which Hume attributed to promises is found in all three things. A promise is naturally unintelligible because when I promise I am supposed to create a necessity, say for me to do something. This happens (in suitable circumstances) by my telling someone that I will; or, again, by some feature of the way I speak in doing so. The explanation of the feature is precisely that it signifies imposing the necessity! But what kind of necessity is it? Some kinds of necessity we may derive from observation of nature, perhaps, but not this one. Yet it is produced. But what is produced is not an independently describable effect, as it were magically brought about by signs. It does not exist at all except for the signs. It is as if words produced it by signalling it; but what do they signal except the future action? The extra thing remains unexplained.

The parallel for rights will become clear a little later. Meanwhile, we may note that no useful definition of a right can be given. But definition is not the only mode of explanation. The thing to consider is modals.

Modals come in related pairs, the necessity modal and the possibility modal. What is common to all types is that the two modals of a given pair are mutually interdefinable. The actual use of modals is rather wider than we usually take account of in philosophy. The first extension of consideration in modern philosophy beyond logical and natural necessity and possibility was made by the investigation of so-called 'deontic logic'. In ancient times, Aristotle in his *Metaphysica*, made the pregnant remark that one sense of "necessary" is *that without which some good will not be obtained or some evil averted*.

There is in fact a huge array of uses of modals, of can, can't, need, need not, has to, doesn't have to, is free to, is not free to, must, must not, ought, need not, necessary, possible, together with the modal inflections of other words. In Latin and Greek there is a necessity inflection of verbs as well as a possibility inflection; in some modern languages only the latter. When it is said categorically that something must be, or has to be, or can't but be, sometimes it is important for the correctness of this that it *is* then; sometimes that it *is* later; sometimes neither matters for the correctness of the 'must'. Examples of the first: "John must be in the kitchen", "The Prime Minister has to live in Downing Street". Of the second: "All we humans alive now have to die", "Surely N must win (can't lose)!" Of the third: "She must be given plenty of fluids", "You have to move your king". These types are a tiny selection.

Among the many many uses of modals we notice a range of uses which may be brought under the heading: "stopping from doing something". One might mention ones that are used to make people do things too; but in approaching the topic of rights I am interested in what I will call "stopping modals" e.g. "You can't move your king". Someone may want to say that the latter means "Moving your king in this situation is against the rules". So it does. But one may equally well say: "That's against the rules" is *a* special form of "you can't do that". Think how a child learns to play chess. It grasps the idea of a rule partly from this use of "you can't". After all what it 'can't' do, in another sense it perhaps plainly *can*, if you don't physically stop it. But these utterances first accompany other methods of preventing or stopping an action, and then by themselves they function to prevent or stop it. With one set of circumstances (including consequences) this business is part of the build-up of the concept of a rule; in another, of that of a piece of etiquette; in another, of that of a promise, in another of an act of sacrilege, etc. It is characteristic of human intelligence to be able to learn the response to a stopping modal without which it could not exist as a linguistic form.

Naturally stopping cannots are compatible with – i.e. are to be found unfaulted with – the actual occurrence of what 'cannot' be. Except in the following type of case: where what 'cannot' be is, say, some move in a game then what is actually done if the person isn't stopped by "you can't . . ." is not *called* a move in the game.

Now in the practice of human language and life stopping modals are often used with special mention of persons. "you can't do that, it might hurt Mary"; "You can't sit there, it's John's place"; "You can't eat that, it's for N", "You can't do that, it's for N to do"; "You can't go there, it's N's field"; "You mustn't do that, it will help/damage N"; "You mustn't do that,

N wouldn't like it"; and many others like them. They are extremely various. "You can't eat that, it's for N" stops you, perhaps, with the determination of the speaker that N is going to have it. "It's for N to do" might be connected with tones of contempt for a despised task, and remarks assigning N to a degraded class, or again with respect for N's competence – he knows how, and will do it properly.

But this expression "It's for N to do" might be connected with something different. Take this case: N does not 'have to' do it. No one uses such a formula or even tries to get him to do it. But he is among those who 'can': that is, there are no 'stopping cannots' for him here either way. But if *you* set out to do it, the utterance "you can't, it's for N to do" is followed up with, say, affronted behaviour on N's part, or on his behalf; or fear of the same if you *do* do it. And you may 'have to' make it up to N for having done what was his, not yours, to do. The connection with him is given, not only as a reason for the 'stopping cannot' about your doing it, but also and especially about stopping him from doing it. And it is something that one might very much want to do, either naturally or because it is invested with desirability and dignity by these practices.

Now we can see the similarity to Hume's problem about promises. For what *is* the connection, which is given as a reason? It cannot be explained. This fact is obscured if, as often, there are also substantive connections – such-and-such an object was produced by N, or is used by N, these are N's children, and so on. But they are not *this* connection, and *it is itself nothing, except that it is linguistically MADE.*

Here is (at least in embryo) the idea of 'a right'. The reasons why it is at once so clear and so inexplicable are these: it is clear because we have learned to respond to these stopping cannots, to comply with them, to issue them ourselves, to infringe them. It is inexplicable because, look as we may, we cannot find an *interpretation* of this 'cannot', just as we couldn't find any interpretation of the peculiar 'necessity' (called "obligation") generated by promising. The truth is: there is no interpretation to give, in any of these cases. If we used the language with conviction we 'believed in' the cannots: but what were we believing? We say we are believing in rights – but what sort of thing was that? In the case of games the situation was easier to comprehend: except among the very young, passionate conviction doesn't come into "You can't move the King". Or, if it does, it is conviction about what the rules are. Not about a, so to speak, metaphysical existence of a rule. Questions are usually easily settled by looking in a book. We know it's a matter of convention.

It may seem surprising that I so describe rights: I may seem rather to be describing privileges. But it isn't so. Suppose that, as we say, every man has 'a right' of quiet possession (i.e. occupation) of his home, and suppose the happy situation that everyone *has* a home. Then those stopping cannots will apply to others' (total) use of N's home as N uses it. N alone is free from restriction by those stopping cannots addressed to others in respect of doing there what he 'can' do there. The stopping cannots addressed to everyone else surround and protect his 'can'. Again, my right not to be molested is not a privilege. What does it amount to? It's 'mine' to be where I happen to be in that you 'cannot' simply thrust me out of my path. This is my voting paper – you 'cannot' snatch and mark it. And so on.

The passionate conviction about these cans and cannots – is it based on illusion? Well, what really is the illusion? Let us remember that in many cases a question about just such modal statements is to be settled comparably to the way of settling a question about a rule in chess. For it may be a matter of law. However complex, tortuous and expensive the enquiry, from our present point of view that doesn't make it essentially different. Nor does the fact that opinions may be ambiguous in the end. Again, it may be a matter of prescription: what is the custom among our tribe? Must the juniors stand back and let the seniors go in first? That, let us say, *is* the custom. We may or may not want to erode it. We may want to extinguish a former right on the part of those people, to create a new right for these, by a new practice. And here someone may manifest superstition by insisting that the eroded right is really, so to speak, an invulnerable truth.

But we have not yet asked the serious question, I mean the *grave* question. Here, according to our account, is a concept created by certain linguistic practices. I don't mean by the practice merely of uttering words in a particular arrangement or of doing so in a particular context, but by *actions* (of stopping from doing something) into which words were inserted in such a way that the use of the words themselves became such an action. And not only is the concept created by these practices, these actions with language; it is necessarily created for any particular set of people by a particular set of such practices. Those whose practices they are make or maintain just those rights as the customary rights in their society, only by their having just these practices. Where then are we ever going to be able to argue that what is counted as a right is no right, and something not counted as a right is after all a right? It seems that the question of the *rights of man* falls to the ground! Truth about rights seems to fall into two kinds: what we may call theoretical, scientific truth on the one hand, which will be sociological or anthropological, and on the other statements *within* the practice and the law of a certain society, statements in which we are going along with the language and continuing the practices which create the concept of a right and the particular rights together. A new statement of a right hitherto not acknowledged in the practice of the society can only be a proposal, and the idea of its really being a proposal which accords with an 'abstract truth' about rights must be the merest superstition.

Yet I said that in speaking of authority in connection with government we must speak of a right. How do I stand in so speaking? Am I noticing a practice, or proposing one? If the first, the whole old style search for a justification has got lost; if the second, who am I to make proposals? Am I not merely manifesting my own feelings, perhaps my 'moral' feelings, while falsely pretending to be maintaining a truth, every time I say any such thing as: "Whatever the custom, such-and-such could not be by right" or "Government is distinguished from control by bandits, because government has a right"?

I have often experienced a painful feeling of weakness in offering detailed arguments that such-and-such could not but be unjust, such-and-such could not but be an infringement of rights, this other thing could not but be, say, an act of murder, such-and-such in turn could not be an exercise of authority. They have fallen dead to the ground.

Having reached the beginnings of an account of a right, I see what suggests the impossibility of justifying such statements. Nevertheless, the suggestion is false.

I have located the generation of the concept of a right in a certain kind of use of a stopping modal with what appears to be a reason attached: the reason says that something is N's, or is 'of N', or 'for N'. Note that "being N's" does not signify property, which is merely one case among a host of others. We have here a very special use of the name of a person, or a very special way of relating something to a person, which explains (not is explained by) the general term "right". Something is N's to do, N's to receive (as: a message) N's to kill — as an ancient Roman would say about N's children: the *patria potestas*. The general term "right" is constructed because, as it were, our language feels the need for it. As, for example, a general term "relation" was invented.

At the level of generation of the concept of a right, all rights are necessarily prescriptive and in this sense rights are wholly based upon custom. The existence of such a thing as rights consists in the regular existence of certain proceedings, certain reactions, an integral part of which is the use of certain linguistic forms.

The form of statement 'it's N's' has a peculiar role. It appears to be the form of a reason. Certainly a statement of this form is 'a reason' in the sense of a *logos*, a thought of some kind. But if we ask what the thought is, and for what it is a reason, in: "you can't . . ., it's N's", we find that we cannot explain these independently. We can't explain the "you can't . . ." on its own; in any independent sense it is simply not true that he can't. But neither does "it's N's" have its peculiar sense independent of its relation to this "you can't". That doesn't mean that, once there are these linguistic practices, we can't detach "It's N's" and put it in another context, where it appears distinctly as a reason: "I didn't . . . because it's N's." Let me restrict the word "reason" in this subject matter to something independent which someone actually uses as his reason for an act or abstention. So "I didn't . . . because it's N's to . . ." contains a statement of a reason; the sense that the statement makes is independent of its being a reason. But in "you can't . . . it's N's to . . ." I shall call the particular content of "It's N's to . . ." the *special logos* of the "you can't . . .". My reason for introducing this peculiar terminology is this: I call the second half of the utterance the *logos* of the first because, as I have explained, they are not independent of one another, and I call the particular content the *special logos* because we have a general *logos*-type, with many kinds – diverse particular contents (as: "It's N's to kill or bring up his own child"; "It's N's chair to sit in"). The general type of *logos* gives the formal character of the "you can't . . .", and a general type is always exemplified in a special *logos* of that type. The general type here is the type: a right. But remember that that is not an explanation of the type, it is rather a label for it. Another general type of *logos* is: a rule of a game, which gives the formal character to the "you can't . . ." of "you can't move the King". In "You can't move the King, he'd be in check", "he'd be in check" gives the *special logos* of the "you can't".

Now since a *logos*, thus explained, is a thought, it can be argued about, discussed, reason can be sought for it, reason can be offered against it. Let us take an example:

(1) You can't destroy that, it's a message for N, and he hasn't seen it yet (won't get it if you destroy it).

which is closely connected with:

(2) You can't destroy that, it's for N to get a message which has been sent to him.

In (1) of course, the "you can't" is not necessarily fixed as having the formal character of the stopping modal associated with infringement of rights. It might be the quite different stopping modal exemplified in "You can't move that, the shelf will fall down". In (2) it *is* fixed as the kind of stopping modal we are concerned with – and that *might* be the intent of (1). But on the face of it the difference between (1) and (2) exemplifies the difference between 'fact' and 'right'. (As in '*de facto*' and '*de iure*'.)

Someone to whom (2) is addressed may of course just go ahead and destroy the message; he has, we may suppose, a contempt for the consideration. That is not to argue with it, but merely not to let it weigh with him. But, as I said, it can be argued with. One argument might be that what was stated in (1) was not true. That would not interest us much. Nor would an argument (say "Why should I care? I . . .") for disregarding the consideration in (2). What interests us is an argument against the consideration in (2). The mere facts that (as we will suppose) a use of some such particular stopping modal (about messages) is standard practice in the society, and that if there were no such thing as practices of this general character there would be no such thing as rights among humans at all – these facts do not show that someone cannot argue with the *logos* in (2). What form, then, might our man's argument take? Perhaps "No, it isn't: N is a prisoner", or "a lunatic" or "a child", "a woman" or "my wife", or "my enemy" or "N intends harm and will be helped by this". Or the same things about the sender of the message. If he reasons like this, he seems to be making an exception to some general rule of right. He may however merely be *pointing out* that N, or the particular message, does not fall under the actually current rule of right.

Certainly general rules of right seem to be implicit in this linguistic practice with stopping modals. It is so simply because there has to be a practice. Of course some general rule of right may relate to only one person as the bearer of the right, in connection with whom the same matter often crops up. But it is natural that there should often be general terms in the *logos* which are used similarly in reference to other people besides N.

Our man may be proposing to create new exceptions or to modify the current general rule of right, and in support of this he may produce various arguments. These might be about the ill consequences of including such-and-such types of people in the general rule, or about the inner meaning of the rule (like the 'intent' of a statute) understanding of which will make us 'see' that these people don't fall under it. Or he may attack the whole rule root and branch as doing nothing but harm or as 'senseless'. "Why should mere . . . mean that one can . . .; that equally or more valuable people should have to yield place in . . .?" Thus the qualification referred to in the *logos* may be rhetorically belittled; the disadvantages to those not so qualified rhetorically enlarged upon. Qualifications may obviously be of the most diverse kinds, as: that a man has made a certain journey; has received a special designation; has a particular origin; has had certain marks made on his body; or was born with them; is a sick person; is insane; is a child; is old; is married; is not married; is not a foreigner. It is evident that argument against a general rule of right which belongs to one's tribe's customs can so far hardly take the form of a *proof* of no-right, unless conceding a right to one involves infringing the right of another, and the latter is already of greater weight. That is to say, with the means so far considered, we cannot envisage any other style of proof that a prescriptive right is no right.

There is however one path here. If someone has a role or function which he 'must' perform, or anything that he 'has' to do, then you 'cannot' impede him. Where necessity does not imply actuality, then "necessity implies possibility" may acquire a rather rich significance. This has been noticed before, witness the discussions of "ought implies can". The interesting thing is the switch, as in that case, *from one type of modal* for 'necessity' *to a different type* for 'possibility'. "Ought implies can" is true, if true, however, only in as much as physical impossibility lets one off the hook of blame for something.[2] The crossing of modals that we are considering is more interesting. For any modal, of course "necessarily" is equivalent to "not possibly not" within the same type of modality: hence we may have an interpretation of "must" as "having no right not to". But that case is not one to interest us, it gets us no forrader. One interesting case is, e.g., the "must" that is said by someone who threatens someone else with penalties if something is not done. Now if

---

[2] I mean that, in my opinion, its more interesting interpretation is a falsehood. Namely, that the proof that I 'ought' to do something is sufficient also to prove that I 'can', i.e. that my freedom of will is such that I can.

he also does not allow something without which, it is well understood, what he demands cannot be done, his demands are against reason. That does not mean that they cannot in fact be made; his aim after all may be to push into an 'impossible position', to punish or humiliate. The unreason is not a proof of mistake or stupidity; it may be quite cynical. But it remains unreason.

If any conjunction of modals of different type can be shown to be against reason in this fashion, then we have the materials for a disproof of it, and so we may be able to disprove one of the conjuncts. And this gives us a way of arguing for a right without appeal to custom, law or contract; and similarly of arguing that some customary right is no right but is, rather, a customary wrong. If something is necessary, if it is for example a necessary task in human life, then a right arises in those whose task it is, to have what belongs to the performance of the task. "A right" is of course to be explained as I have explained right, by reference to a certain sort of stopping modal, a set of "you cannots" which surrounds, fixes and protects a 'can' on the part of the one who is thereby said to have a right. The interesting point is precisely that the notion of necessity involved is not the correlate of the 'can' which expresses a right; it is not the equivalent of "no right not to". On the contrary, the necessity takes us out of the circle it is so easy to get into. The necessity, for example, may be human need. As: those who have and carry out the task of bringing up children quite generally perform a necessary task. It cannot be done without children's obedience. So those people have a right to such obedience. My contention is that this is a correct argument, but that it can't be analytically understood without the considerations about modals that I have just put forward. Of course it can be very readily understood at an ordinary common-sense level, but that isn't good enough for us philosophers. This is not mere conceit on our part: the requisite forms of speech would not exist without the practice I have described, and anyone will be at a loss if asked to explain. He has to explain *that* modals are involved, and *how* there is such a use of them. Justification by necessity (of a goal, and of the means to it) is one of the most common – and most commonly abused – forms of justification offered. One might ask: what has 'necessity' got to do with *justification?* The 'necessity' of the goal is very likely the suspicious term of the argument. But in *form* it is sound enough, if I am right about the relation between 'a right' and certain modals.

One thing remains to be said about the notion of a 'task', because it may be a partly modal notion itself. A task, as it is sometimes spoken of, is work which it is in some sense necessary should be done. It may for example be necessary in the sense of being imposed. Or it may be necessary because of a general or particular human need that it should be done. Such a task may not be anyone's task. Someone's task is work which it is necessary that *he* should do or work which it is necessary that someone should do and which it is his right to do. Someone might perform a task which was not his task, which he has even no right to do. Therefore the mere fact that someone is performing a task does not suffice to prove that he has a right to what is needed for the performance of the task. It must either be necessary that he should perform the task or be his right to do it, before he can derive a right to certain things from the fact that they are necessary for the performance of the task. This is needed if we are to use our explanation of a right and yet to derive a right from the necessity of a task. For we shall not get the "you cannot . . . it's N's to . . ." simply from the fact that what N is doing is necessary for someone to do. Unless, indeed, by prescription they say that in N's society; that is, it might be customary to have this sort of stopping modal about impeding anyone who was performing a necessary task, and about trying to take the task from him. Otherwise, before we can argue from performance to right we shall need an argument for particular types of task, that whoever does perform these acquires a right to perform them, or produces a necessity that he should perform them. These considerations have an obvious bearing on situations where some people are performing the functions of government, but without right. That is, they do have such a bearing if there is such a right on the part of governments as we want to find. To that question we must now address ourselves.

III

Frame the Utopian picture if you will. But now add that some people will use violence against others, and will violently resist the decisions and rules. What follows about how this should be reacted to?

Anyone, it may be said, may justly intervene with violence to resist violence committed without right. That is: it can be no infringement of the right of one so resisted. Were it counted one, that would be conceding a right in his violence. (Except on the assumption that any violence against anyone is *eo ipso* an infringement of a right of his.)

So, it may be said, anyone may protect the top decision making authority, and it may protect itself with a regular force. Such a force may also ward off attack on other people and activities.

Even in respect of protection against violence, the state goes far beyond this. We have pictured something like a business's employing guards for its own direct protection, and extending their services to the direct protection of others. But the civil authority investigates past actions; tries and punishes people, and forces rules on them.

This would be an insolent claim on the part of any 'private' corporation. When these things are done with the authority of government, it seems we have a transition to a new kind of thing.

In fact we went absurdly far with the right to protect oneself and others against violence, though even so it got us nowhere near civil authority. The regular force for protecting the offices, etc., of the authority – how are we to picture it intervening *ad hoc* to protect the unjustly attacked? On whose side do they intervene? The role of the civil power in using a standing force cannot be assimilated to that of a passer-by who sees someone set on by a thug.

This is one of the fundamental questions of political theory: are we to understand civil *authority* as arising by a transfer of rights already possessed by men without a state? Those who maintain this always assume a private right of punishment in a state of nature. We deny this and take the alternative view: civil society is the bearer of rights of coercion not possibly existent among men without government.

A standing force that systematically has the protective task must be an intervening force to stop or prevent violence, and bring the parties to a place of judgement, not itself the on-the-spot judge of issues. Judgement is needed; this requires procedures for determining which disputants shall succeed. The question "with what right?" asked about the action of the intervening force could have the answer that it was a customary right: this office exists and is generally acknowledged in the society. *Now* our picture is that of violence being checked and quarrels turned into 'civil dispute'. We haven't envisaged any way of enforcing decisions. The method might work – because people commonly accepted the decision – in a rather special community. But in a large natural society it could hardly be enough.

Thus we approach the necessity of laws in connection with the protective role of a standing force. The force is no longer neutral. There is trial and punishment. 'Law' here need not be statutory but must be positive: it is in this context the at least customary and also manifest prohibition of various wrongs – and so far we are considering only wrongs of violence. There needs to be place for complaint of one man against another in respect of prohibited wrongs.

The justification falls into two parts. First, are those who are punished wronged by it? To this the answer is: evidently not, in the sense of getting what they don't deserve, in respect of their primary affliction. That is if the victims are the intended ones. If the conceptions of guilt and responsibility that operate are correct ones, they are not wronged in what I'll call the primary way, namely by getting punished without desert. But there is a second question, which concerns the right to give deserved affliction. One may be wronged in a secondary way by getting one's deserts at the hands of someone who had no right so to inflict them.

This part of the justification of the institution of law, trial and punishment resides only in its necessity for the protection of people. *It* cannot reside in mere custom. Here I will offer the promised calculation, whereby the right of government itself cannot be merely a customary right. Wherever we have what purports to be a customary right, let us form the hypothesis that those who are directly disadvantaged or damaged by its exercise are thereby wronged. If, if the damage is a wrong it is a great wrong, then the purported customary right itself can be no right but is rather a customary wrong. Now someone who is punished for wrongs that he commits by one who has no right to punish him gets at least as great a wrong as the damage counts as, that he suffers.

Test this on wrongs which no one does have a customary or legal or contractual right to punish, and where a right to punish cannot be derived from need: assume that the damage inflicted is of a kind that does count as a wrong if inflicted without right.

The justification of the institution of trial and punishment thus has to be based on need, not on prescription. With this is settled the wearisome dispute about the different theories of punishment by public authority: retributive, deterrent and reformatory. A retributive theory of punishment is merely a punishment theory of punishment; therefore correct, in that it declares that nothing can be properly called punishment if it is not offered as affliction deserved by ill-doing; but incorrect, in that it says that punishment of wrongdoing is *eo ipso* justified and needs no further reason. The deterrent theory is often discussed – and berated – in quasi-forgetfulness that it is a theory of the justification of *punishment* by civil authority. To be that, it must be a theory of putting affliction on people for something they have done, and therefore, if it is to be just at all the 'something' must be a known offence and the punishment deserved. Granted that, the deterrent theory is the correct one. For even if (which one may doubt) there is something intrinsically good about an evil-doer's suffering, what is one man or some set of men that they should bring this about? Are they so good themselves? and are they in charge of the order of things, to see to it that such a good is brought about? It is obvious nonsense. The justification of the institutions of law, charge, trial and sentence can only be the protection of people. This cannot be supposed to be its effect but by potential wrongdoers being restrained by the terror of the law. For this, we need the assumption that without the law there would be a lot more of that wrong-doing than there is with it. – The reformatory theory assimilates the state to a parent. In itself this is a monstrous impertinence. For it means that purely in virtue of the position of holding civil power, some men may claim to dispose of others in this way against their wills for their own good. Upholders of the 'reformatory' idea, or the idea of 'rehabilitation' are probably confused about this, not noticing the actual character of the claim; but they may be motivated by a certain sweetness. The good in their idea is the good of the injunction: "Do not forget, even in punishing him, that the convict is your brother, now in your power: do not become callous about *his* good." They take it for granted that they – or 'we' – have a right to decide 'what to do with criminals'. The question is, how such a right can exist? By my calculation, it cannot be just a customary right.

A parallel argument for the right of punishment could not supply the defects in e.g., Locke's argument[5] and so show that men in a state of nature may – nay it is needful that they should – severally punish those who unjustly attack them and their neighbours. For action on such a principle will perforce be action against those whom a man believes so to deserve punishment. His formation of opinion then takes the place of trial in our account.

[5] Locke's argument depends on assuming a Law of Nature; he argues that, like any other law, it must have sanctions. But if the legislator does not speedily punish transgressions of the law, it is not clear why we may.

In consequence of such formation of opinion he is going to do some attacking himself. But on the same principle those who think otherwise than he will then equally attack him. And so instead of procuring a peaceful normality, such a principle would promote a general warfare within which even the quietest (namely, those who failed in that duty of punishing unjust attackers) could hardly hope to go safely. Hence I denied that right of punishment.

Nor is the ground of necessity an unsafe one in that there are no limits to what can be 'justified' by necessity, if anything can. For the necessity of the arrangement was not the whole justification. It was assumed that the wronger of others suffered a *condign* punishment. In the primary way, then, he is not wronged but, if he is wronged he is wronged in the secondary way because the inflicter of desert had no right to inflict it. It is only at this point that necessity is invoked as a justification. Nor is necessity the justification in the particular case. *There* the justification is the particular law, the citation of which in justification is an aspect of the institution of law with its enforcement. So the institution is what is justified – and only at this point of the argument – by necessity.

The institution creates the character of an act as one of *doing justice on* the wronger of others, which character was not guaranteed by an act's being an act of afflicting the wrongdoer not contrary to desert.

In this way we have the genesis of a quite new kind of right, something new has emerged. If we have this institution, we have civil society with civil government and its authority, and if not, not.

To take stock, and see gaps, consider the following objections. First, we have concentrated too much on protection against violence. There is as much need of protection against fraud. Second, we are being unhistorical, and influenced by the characteristic claim of a modern state to a monopoly of violence.

Taking the second first: it is true that there may be a state with laws, none of which generally prohibits violence. Unrestricted violence is not tolerated in any society, but violence may be left to be partly restricted by social disapproval and by strong men; for the rest, it may be regarded as a sort of brawling which no one interferes with. The laws all concern, say, status and its obligations and rights, property, marriage, jurisdiction, contracts. You strike your neighbour and damage him: that's between him and you (or your families). If you move his landmark, fail in some due, usurp his function, he can complain of you before judges. Corporations also have many rights, and they will take you to court if they can claim you have infringed them. All this may strike us as strange, but it is possible: the people of such a society might regard us as obsessed with protection against violence: this is either unmanly concern or the matter is just the concern of heads of great households. Of course killing one man may be regarded as damage to another, and claim for damages may lie, as among the Anglo-Saxons. But there is not a direct law against murder, mayhem and blows. Strong men are able to help themselves and their dependants! The protection of the law is needed for quite other purposes.

It is quite true: we cannot say that there is no state (no government), where there is not legal protection against personal violence. But I have not said this. We *can* say that one of the principal things that people in general need governments (governmental violence) for *is* protection against violence. If many must rely for this on 'strong men' whose clients or serfs they thus become, they are at the mercy of the strong men themselves. The need of systematic protection, I argued, involves a need for laws, trials and punishment in the matter; a need, in short, for an administration of justice. And I further said that having 'this institution', i.e. an administration of justice, was involved in there being civil government and civil authority. But this does not imply that there is civil government and civil authority only where there are laws against murder and assault.

The other objection related to people's having as great a need to be protected against fraud as against violence. The claim is specious, I suspect, because "fraud" sounds like a clear-cut notion covering a large number of actions that one may need protection from. And this in turn is because "fraud" is a legal term of enormously wide application. Legally understood, it seems to be applied to pretty well any criminally or civilly wrongful act by which one person is prejudiced through the deception of another. But it is not applicable *unless* the act is legally wrongful. I might lyingly tell someone that Roman remains have been found in my neighbour's garden, and that I am not interested, but that if he cares to dig up my garden, he can have any that he finds. My garden is a mere section of field and I am much pleased when it gets thoroughly dug over. Would that be fraud? Not legally. Now, if one isn't relying on legal notions of fraud, how can one specify the need for protection against fraud? Is there a general need of protection against ruses? The idea is absurd.

What has to be said is: people need protection against some infringements of rights by deception. And: they need protection against being deceived in going through various transactions, usually though not always already legally characterized (conveyancing, for example). The protection here takes the form of allowing the invalidation of such transactions on grounds of fraud. But the relevance of the authority to use coercive force which is characteristic of the state lies far in the background in these cases, at least where there is no question of criminal prosecution. In a society with a legal system people want and need certain things for which there are legal forms, and in some cases the very things that they want are legal facts, such as entitlement, letters of administration, powers of attorney, discharges of various kinds. The protection from fraud that is in question is then not a protection by the force in the hand of the rulers, it is a protection by legal provision and practice from being entrapped through fraud in undesired legal states of affairs. These no doubt usually have solid material consequences. But the whole possibility of the fraud from which protection is needed in such cases is not one which could arise and threaten you in a state of nature. There is thus something confusing and misleading about putting force and fraud together as two equal things the need of protection from which gives a foundation for civil authority. The scope for fraud, of kinds that laws directly protect one from, is relatively limited in a state of nature.

What should be said, rather, is that in any human society of many families, there will be institutional practices, conventions and customary rights. Of these latter, some may be quite simple to give an account of, as: a right to fish a certain stretch of river. Whereas others are connected with very complex practices, as: a right, perhaps unique to an individual, to wear something or to make a quite particular mark somewhere. The exercise of such rights may have considerable practical consequences, and their existence be important instruments in living. (Think for example of signing one's name.)

Now when this is so, and when there are great numbers of people, mostly not knowing one another but in fair proximity, customary rights will be protected by a system in which power (involving a threat of coercive force) is exercised over people; complaint of infringements may be made, issues decided by customary methods and according to customary principles, disputing parties have a solution laid down for them, accused people found guilty or not guilty, and the convicted punished. I say it will be so because it will be so if the people are to continue in the exercise of customary rights. Extinction of these by disorder, the 'war of everyone against everyone' or again by enslavement by conquerors, is of course also possible.

It is possible in a relatively small population that power and these judgements should be exercised by a general assembly operating by majority vote. That makes no difference to the point that concerns us. If such exercise of power and judgement is a regular institution of the society, then it has the essential mark of a civil society with laws. There we have civil authority. In the case just imagined the majority (severally) obey the majority (collectively). Since the orders and decisions may concern now one man now another, the majority may obey not only severally but for the most part piecemeal, in respect of different matters and at different times and in different places. As we have imagined the case, they obey under the implicit institutional threat of coercion, perhaps from a section of the population (whose office it is). This section acts against the few who choose not to obey. They have, it may be presumed, commanding officers, and there is some method by which they are formally cognisant of the decision of the assembly which they have to enforce.

It is of course true that the whole business rests on consent. But not much more so than any civil government does. Government always rests on consent in the sense that it could not exist without at least the passive consent of a large majority. Or (in the very rare cases) the extremely active and lively consent of a large minority who keep the others down. I am thinking here of the Spartans and the Helots; each Spartan lad did active service in the field, living incognito among the Helots and murdering any who looked as if they might get uppity. *That* I do not call passive consent of the majority! In the case that I have imagined, if the whole or nearly the whole adult population go to the assembly, the consent of the majority (severally) to the decisions is perhaps not so passive as if they were not members of the assembly. What there is active consent to, and that simply by participation, is the procedure for deciding and judging. But we must not forget that "the" majority is not a particular set of people consenting severally to what they have all voted for. It is possible that, although every decision has been made by majority vote, the majority votes in the minority in a majority of cases. Let there be an assembly of ten voting (all of them) on a set of decisions, each of which especially affects one of them:

	A	B	C	D	E	F	G	H	I	J
Decision on										
A	0	0	0	1	1	0	1	1	1	1
B	0	0	0	1	1	1	1	1	1	0
C	0	1	0	1	1	1	1	1	0	0
D	1	1	1	0	1	0	1	1	0	0
E	0	0	0	1	0	1	1	1	1	1
F	0	0	0	1	1	0	1	1	1	1
G	1	1	1	1	1	0	0	1	0	0
H	1	0	1	1	1	0	1	0	0	1
I	1	1	0	1	1	0	1	1	0	0
J	0	0	1	1	1	1	1	1	0	0

Here A, B, C, F, I and J all vote in the majority only four times out of the ten. Everyone votes in the minority on the matter that especially affects himself. It doesn't seem reasonable to say that 'the majority', in going along with the decisions of 'the majority', is merely going along with itself. Although A, B, C, F, I and J have been active in voting one may still reasonably call their acceptance passive consent. The illusion of not being subject to an authority exercising power over one might prevail where one had voted with the majority, but it would be none the less an illusion.

Thus an assembly can be sovereign over all the members of a population, who are its subjects, even when it is constituted by all of them together. It can of course make law for its own action and methods of procedure, as well as for every member of itself. In the former case it is inappropriate to speak of 'it' as obeying itself; for in that case the law is made for its collective proceedings, and 'it' rather adheres to its law, which 'it' can change, than obeys it. But in respect of the individuals who are severally subject to the laws, decisions and verdicts, as also to the laws made for the actions and procedures of the assembly itself, the concept of obedience to commands promulgated by authority is perfectly applicable. Hart, who attacks the notions of 'sovereign' and 'subject' where we have a democracy,[4] has many reasonable things to say about rules. But he seems to think that his account

[4] *The Concept of Law* (Oxford, 1961), p. 74.

of rules and of proceeding according to them is in competition with the conception of sovereign and subject. How could that be so? In a small and intimate group, there might be an autocratic father or leader giving direct orders *ad hoc* to everyone, and in consequence no institutional rules may be needed except those of language itself. But in a larger society, even with a single autocratic dictator, there must be such rules as Hart discusses.

What counts as an order or permission from the dictator? Who are his agents and officers? What are the credentials by which they may be known? Etc.

This consideration of how the concepts of sovereign and subject still stand in the purest imaginable sort of democracy was something of a digression. I will take up the thread of my argument. There is no civil government except where there are laws, however these arise or are made. Laws entail an 'administration of justice' under which there (1) can be accusations of infringement of the laws themselves, or (2) can be complaints (in respect of wrongs) and claims (in respect of rights). In either case the justification is the need for protection of the sort afforded by laws and the power of enforcing them.

The idea of civic authority, so far as it threatens coercion against *any* defiance of laws (no matter what they may be) seems to pull itself up by its bootstraps. The threatened violence cannot be just except against the man who is acting unjustly; he is acting unjustly if he is defying the law, but the sanction of force behind the laws is just only against the unjust. Which comes first, the injustice of the man the civic authority threatens, or the law? If the injustice of the man, how can he threatened merely because he defies a law? If he is unjust *because* he defies the law, what gave the law this position, of something that could be sustained with the threat of force?

The answer to this is that we have to take two bites at the cherry. First, there is both a very general need of protection of life and limb against violence, *and* a need of protection of some customary rights. We have seen that there may be, indeed have been, legal systems that met the second need and not the first. We can then ask whether any of those over whom the civil power claims authority are without substantial rights which it protects? If so, then its claim to authority over them has no foundation at all. They are not among those whose needs are met.

So much for our first bite. At this stage the answer to the question "which comes first?" is "the injustice of the man the law threatens".[5] We will call the laws in question the 'primary' laws.

Now for the second bite. We saw and granted the need of a top decision-making machinery in a large complex society. Our *problem* concerned the right to coerce people who refused to accept the decisions. *The right could not derive directly from the need of this machinery for the general good.* For if for the sake of the general good it is proposed to damage my interests and erode or ex-

---

[5] Except in a special case, where there are people who have no customary rights which are infringed by casually killing them, though there is not supposed to be a customary right of killing them either. I will not go into this here for lack of space.

tinguish some of my customary rights, and I shall be subjected to force if I don't go along with this, the question arises: why should I respect the decision? It becomes a mere conflict of interests, with the more powerful clobbering the weaker, unless we can show an authority to impose the decisions on me. There has to have arisen a customary right to obedience, which customary right can then be protected by law. In our original construction we identified the top decision-makers with the people commanding protection of the whole top-decision-making machinery, who extended this protection to everyone's life and limb considered severally. This identified them with those responsible for the administration of justice, which was especially connected with the protection of people against violence. We have seen that the administration of justice *may* not be concerned with that. But the relevant identification will occur anyway. Those by whose authority the primary laws are enacted (1) acquire a customary right to obedience and (2) exercise, and therefore have, a good deal of power. It is thus very natural that they should extend their activities, perform the work of arbitration, make many decisions affecting now this now that section of the population, and promote as well as lending countenance to many large enterprises. If they *obtain* obedience in doing these things, such obedience is likely to become to some extent and in some contexts a customary right. That is does so is of course a result of the response of the people who accept the decisions. Then, either through more legal practice or through enactment, the right gets protected by laws. The right explicitly to make laws becomes a customary right – through being exercised without too much check or set-back. And here the answer to the question: which comes first, the injustice of the action of the man whom the law threatens, or the law? is: the law. The law creates the injustice of the man who breaks it.

We have to ask: how does the supposed customary right to obedience fare under the critical calculation which I offered? The answer is naturally not a simple failure or a simple success for custom. It evidently depends on what people are required to be obedient to. Thus, though the law creates offences, authority to do so is not limitless. We have noted in passing that decisions may *destroy* customary rights. This fact produces a familiar sort of tension between the different functions of government (of the whole apparatus). It may be asked how, on my construction, law can ever extinguish a customary right without thereby committing a wrong. I suppose the answer is that a need can extinguish a right (see Section II for the logic of this) and that those who have the authority to make certain decisions about what is needed thereby acquire a right to extinguish such rights as are extinguishable by needs. This is the source of as many dangers as arguments from necessity are subject to abuses.

Our original question: what distinguishes the authority of government from control by bandits? has received an at least preliminary answer. The distinction lies in the association of government with a system of administration of justice. This, incidentally, shows how the original condition of being run by bandits could actually develop into a situation of having a government.

But there is a change in the reverse direction, which must give us pause. If bandits acquire control, they may after all keep the forms and machinery of the administration of justice in being, and utilize them (Huey Long). And what at one stage is a government, enjoying civic authority, may degenerate into a sort of banditry, equally keeping and utilizing those forms and that machinery. Again, foreign invaders usurping the powers of government will perhaps maintain and utilize those forms and cannot be said thereby straightaway to acquire the authority of legitimate government. It is clear that with the lapse of time, if their 'government' is not then such as to designate them rather as bandits, they do eventually acquire it. So the serious question for us is posed by the first cases.

There is one consideration here which has something like the position of absolute zero or the velocity of light in current physics. It cannot possibly be an exercise of civic authority deliberately to kill or mutilate innocent subjects. The steps are sufficiently obvious, by which we can arrive from the consideration of the questions involved in clarifying this proposition at *this* (rather academic) one: the enactment of a law by which it was an offence to go on living (though one had committed no *other* offence) is not a possibility for legitimate government. The proposition is academic because when governments take to murdering their subjects they seldom make positive law explicitly authorizing the killing. But the academic proposition is of interest to us. The reason for it should be clear from our whole investigation: authority in the command of violence (which was what we first saw as distinguishing government from a Mafia in control of a place) is based on its performance of a task which is a general human need. A way of treating someone which puts him outside the class of those for whom the task is performed puts him outside the class of those subject to the authority. It is arguable that the death penalty for crimes does itself do this, but also arguable (I think successfully) that it does not. But if one's only 'offence' is supposed to be that (being a Welshman, say, or a Gypsy) one continues to exist, then it is clear beyond argument that one is put out of that class and so cannot be guilty under the law purporting to create the offence.

Index